Vegan
love story

Vegan Love Story
First published in English in 2015 by:
New Internationalist Publications,
The Old Music Hall,
106-108 Cowley Road,
Oxford OX4 1JE,
UK

newint.org

New in paperback in 2019

From the original German edition published in 2014 by AT Verlag, Aarau and Munich

Authors: Reto Frei (tibits AG), Rolf Hiltl (Hiltl AG)
Translated from the German by: Quarto Translations
tibits recipes: edited by Gabriel Adé, Patrizia Catalano, Klaus Reiter
Hiltl recipes: edited by Dorrit Türck, Anna Schlatter
Project leader: Annette Gröbly Frei
Concept: Reto Frei, Rolf Hiltl, Annette Gröbly Frei, Marsha Lehmann, Dorrit Türck
Photography/visual concept: Juliette Chrétien, www.juliettechretien.com
Photo and food styling: Karin Frey, www.karinfrey.ch
Photography and food styling assistance: Roman Pulvermüller
Accompanying text (introduction, product pages and portraits): Christian Seiler, www.christianseiler.com
Proofing: Nicola Härms, Rheinbach
Design and layout: Nora Vögeli, www.noravoegeli.com and Amy Guest (cover) and Andrew Kokotka for New Internationalist
Image processing: Vogt-Schild Druck, Derendingen
Dishes and accessories (with a small number of exceptions) were made available with the friendly co-operation of: Caravane, Paris; Rina Menardi, Italy; Potomak, Italy; Coté West Living, Zurich, Switzerland; Globus, Zurich, Switzerland; Mäder Kräuter, Boppelsen, Switzerland.
Printing and binding: APPL, aprinta Druck, Wemding, Germany

British Library Cataloguing-in-Publication Data
A catalogue record for this book is available from the British Library.

Library of Congress Cataloging-in-Publication Data
A catalog record for this book is available from the Library of Congress.

ISBN: 978-1-78026-545-2

HILTL & TIBITS
THE
COOKBOOK

CONTENTS

Introduction: A culinary universe

This is the second book by tibits and the fourth by Hiltl, but the first which these two closely allied family businesses have written together. And it is not a vegetarian, but a vegan cookbook – a book in which the dedication and passion of tibits and Hiltl is demonstrated.

In 80 recipes, a culinary universe is revealed which reflects a modern, intelligent way of life. Many people are vegan because they value healthy and enjoyable food and at the same time have not lost sight of the bigger picture – the world in which we all live.

The environmental and ethical advantages of the vegan diet over a conventional diet have been clear for some time. In light of these indisputable facts, many people simply decide they want no part in the food industry's distribution wars or factory farming and opt instead for a more modern and active way of meeting their nutritional needs. They eat what grows in the garden, or more precisely, what grows in the garden of the world.

The vegan dishes introduced in this book are multicultural in the truest sense: they originate from all corners of the globe. And this in turn reflects the culture of Hiltl and tibits in so many different ways.

First, vegan cuisine has played an important role in the company history of both Hiltl and tibits. In the case of Hiltl, even when it opened in 1898 there were already several vegan dishes on the menu (back then, mostly raw fruit and vegetables), and tibits – which has restaurants in Switzerland, in Germany and in central London – has continuously increased the proportion of vegan dishes on its menu to 85 per cent and rising, without having drawn attention to this.

Second, experimentation in the restaurants' testing kitchens is influenced and inspired by an international cuisine, which is logical given the many culinary cultures that are naturally based on vegetarian and vegan dishes. In addition, up to 50 nationalities are represented among the staff at the two companies, and these employees bring personal preferences and valuable suggestions that make their way into Hiltl and tibits' daily fare.

So if there is a clear trend towards vegan eating at the moment, then tibits and Hiltl may have helped shape this over the last few decades, during which time they supported the development of each individual dish by discussing it in depth with their guests. It was actually these guests who requested that we adapt the vegetarian range of the two restaurants towards the vegan and make available the recipes that resulted for use at home.

With the recipes from this book, you can enjoy yourself without compromising your ethical and environmental principles. Refusing to put the needs of humans above those of nature, *Vegan Love Story* celebrates both natural and cultural diversity. The Hiltl and tibits journey through global vegan delights will conjure a satisfied smile on the reader's face.

Christian Seiler, journalist, columnist and author

Read the Portrait of Hiltl and tibits on page 218.

Refusing to put the needs of humans above those of nature, Vegan Love Story *celebrates both natural and cultural diversity. The Hiltl and tibits journey through global vegan delights will conjure a satisfied smile on the reader's face.*

Hiltl

tibits

STARTERS, APPETIZERS AND SOUPS

Exotic, colourful, healthy:
Getting your meal off
to a flying start

The nutrient suppliers: oils, fats, nuts, and seeds

Nuts and seeds are not only delicious components of our food, but also particularly useful. As well as unsaturated fatty acids, they also supply us with high-quality protein, vitamins and minerals. Vegans obtain a significant part of their nutrients from this food group and should eat at least three tablespoons of these each day.

There is a wide variety. It ranges from **walnuts** through to **pine nuts** and **pumpkin seeds**, from **wheatgerm**, **linseeds** and **hemp seeds** to **sesame** and **chia seeds** – and then extends even further into a range of exotic nuts and seeds. With their irresistible texture and characteristic flavours, they enrich breads, cakes, quiches, rissoles and burgers. A handful of roasted nuts or seeds is often enough to pep up a plate of salad and turn it into a treat.

Just as important to vegans are high-quality vegetable oils, the multiple unsaturated fatty acids within which are essential for the human body. A particularly large amount of the useful omega-3 fatty acids are contained in cold-pressed **hemp seed, linseed, walnut and rapeseed oil**. As hemp seed and linseed oils go off quickly, it is better to buy these in small bottles. The aroma of both oils is usually very striking. If the taste of them is too intense when using it in a salad dressing, mix it with neutral-tasting rapeseed oil. All of these oils work well for cold dishes.

If you plan to use the oil at higher temperatures, you should change your selection. For frying, searing or braising these oils have a high proportion of simple unsaturated fatty acids: **olive, almond, avocado and hazelnut oil**. For roasting, deep-fat frying and baking, so-called HOLL rapeseed oil or HO sunflower oil are suitable. The abbreviations of HOLL and HO stand for 'High Oleic/Low Linolenic' and indicate that the oil has a high proportion of heat-resistant oil acids and a low proportion of heat-sensitive alpha linolenic acids. These oils derive from specially cultivated rapeseed plants or sunflowers and are particularly heat-resistant.

As well as oils for everyday use, there are also countless oils from special nuts and seeds which can be used in small quantities for seasoning.

West Indian Cucumber Soup

Refreshingly exotic!

Preparation time
40 Minutes

Serves 4

½ cucumber
½ small carrot
½ small parsnip
1 floury potato
20 g/4 tsp fresh ginger
2 tsp ground cumin
1 tsp ground turmeric
½ tsp ground asafoetida
2 tbsp neutral-flavoured
vegetable oil
1 tsp brown mustard seeds
1 bayleaf
2 tbsp red lentils
1 litre/4¼ cups vegetable
stock
2 sprigs each of
marjoram and parsley
2 tbsp freshly squeezed
lemon juice
100 ml/7 tbsp orange juice
2 tbsp raw cane sugar
Salt, ground pepper
1 tbsp sesame seeds

Peel the vegetables and the potato and chop them all into 2-cm/¾-inch cubes. Peel the ginger, chop finely and crush with the cumin, turmeric and asafoetida using a pestle and mortar.

Heat the oil in a pan, add the mustard seeds and fry on a low heat while stirring until they crack and produce a delicate fragrance. Add the crushed spices with the bayleaf and the lentils and fry together, stirring occasionally. Add the vegetables and the potatoes and fry on a medium heat for 5 minutes, stirring occasionally, so that the spices do not burn.

Cover with vegetable stock and cook everything at a medium temperature for about 15 minutes, until the vegetables are soft. Remove the bayleaf and purée the soup with the hand blender.

Finely chop the marjoram and the parsley and add to the soup together with the lemon and orange juice and the sugar. Season with salt and pepper. Serve the soup sprinkled with sesame seeds.

TIPS
Instead of the light-coloured sesame seeds, use the aromatic black variety or garnish the soup with a handful of roasted peanuts. This goes well with poppadoms – fried Indian crisps made from legumes. Asafoetida, also known as devil's dirt, is a popular Indian seasoning which can be used as a replacement for garlic. Alternatively, you could use a finely chopped clove of garlic.

Aubergine/Eggplant and Amaranth

A gem from the Andes, prepared just as carefully

Preparation time
35 minutes
(including baking time)

Serves 4

2 aubergines/eggplants
4 tbsp olive oil
200 g/1 cup amaranth
1 sprig parsley
1 sprig basil
1 handful rocket/
arugula plus a few stalks
to garnish

For the dressing
40 ml/4 dessert spoons
vegetable stock
1 tsp chilli oil
2 tbsp white balsamic
vinegar
Salt, ground pepper

Preheat the oven to 200°C/390°F.

Wash and prepare the aubergines/eggplants and then cut into 2-cm/¾-inch cubes. Mix with the olive oil and spread evenly over a baking tray covered with baking paper. Bake in the preheated oven for 15-20 minutes until the cubes are golden brown and soft. Leave to cool on the baking tray.

Rinse the amaranth well under cold running water. Add to boiling water and simmer for about 20 minutes. Drain in a very fine sieve, rinse off and allow to dry completely. Wash the parsley, basil and rocket/arugula, shake dry and chop finely.

Mix together the ingredients for the dressing. Season with salt and pepper. Mix the dried amaranth with the dressing and the chopped herbs. Finally, carefully mix in the diced aubergine/eggplant. Serve on plates or in glasses and garnish with fresh rocket rocket/arugula.

TIPS
This works just as well with pitta bread or as bruschetta. Amaranth is one of the oldest agricultural crops known to humanity and has a particularly high iron and protein content.

Pickled Star Fruit

A crowning glory of finger foods and desserts

Preparation time
30 minutes
+ 30 minutes infusion
time

Serves 4

2 large star fruit
1 lemon
100 g/½ cup sugar
1 pinch saffron threads
1 pinch chilli powder

Cut the star fruit crossways into slices half a centimetre or a quarter-inch thick. Squeeze the lemon.

Put the star fruit in a pan with the lemon juice and half the sugar, pour in 150 ml/⅔ cup of water and bring to the boil. Simmer on a low heat for 5 minutes until the fruit is soft – do not allow the fruit to disintegrate! Lift the fruit out of the liquid with a slotted spoon and remove any remaining cores, then put to one side.

Put the remaining sugar, the saffron threads and the chilli powder into the pan and boil down for about 5 minutes. Put the star fruit back into the liquid and leave to infuse for at least 30 minutes with the hob switched off.

TIPS
Time is needed for the yellow colour of the saffron to develop. This dish is therefore best prepared well in advance. To store pickled fruit, fill jars up to the brim while still hot, seal and turn them upside-down for 5 minutes. This way, they can be kept sealed in the fridge for at least one month.

Miso Soup with Shiitake Mushrooms and Soy Beans

Create a piece of Japan with this light starter!

Preparation time
15 minutes

Serves 4

**For the contents of
the soup**
1 spring onion/scallion
30 g/½ cup shiitake
mushrooms
1 tsp neutral-flavoured
vegetable oil
20 g/2 tbsp fresh or
frozen soy beans

For the soup
80 g/¼ cup white shiro
miso paste
1 tsp soy sauce
400 ml/1⅔ cups
vegetable stock
Salt, ground pepper

For the soup contents, wash and prepare the spring onion/scallion, cut in half and then into fine strips. Wash the shiitake mushrooms and dry with kitchen paper. Then cut into fine strips.

Heat the oil in a small frying pan and sauté the spring onion/scallion and the mushrooms until almost soft. Then add the soy beans and stir through. Put to one side.

For the soup, bring 600 ml/2½ cups of water to the boil in a large pan and add the miso paste, the soy sauce and the vegetable stock. Season with salt and pepper to taste. Put the soup contents into soup bowls and pour over the hot soup.

TIPS
Peas can also be used instead of soy beans. If you would like to serve the soup as a main meal, you could add rice noodles, udon noodles or tofu pieces to the soup contents. Shiro miso (white miso paste) is the white, light variety of miso paste.

Green Tomato Chutney

A wonderful addition to any table

Preparation time
1 hour

Serves 4

6 ripe green tomatoes
1 shallot
1 clove of garlic
20 g/4 tsp fresh ginger
3 small green chillies
100 ml/7 tbsp cider
vinegar
120 g/9 tbsp raw cane
sugar
1 unwaxed lime
1 apple (sharp variety
such as Granny Smith)
1 pinch ground cumin
1 tsp ground turmeric
Salt

TIP
*Fully ripe green tomatoes must
be used for the chutney, and
not unripe red tomatoes. The
green varieties of tomato are
particularly crunchy. The most
well known are Green Zebra,
Green Grape and Evergreen.
These are available at markets,
at specialist greengrocers' and in
well-stocked supermarkets.*

Remove the stalks from the tomatoes, cut a cross into the bottoms and put into boiling water until the skins begin to loosen (this takes longer than with fully ripe red tomatoes). Refresh in cold water and then pull off the skins. Cut the tomatoes into quarters, remove the cores and dice finely. Peel the shallots, garlic and ginger and chop finely. Cut off the stalks of the chillies and cut in half lengthways, remove the centres and cut into fine rings.

Heat the cider vinegar and the sugar in a pan until the sugar has melted. Add the shallots, garlic and ginger and leave to simmer on a medium heat for 10 minutes.

In the meantime, wash the lime in hot water and dry. Grate the zest and squeeze the juice. Peel the apple, cut into quarters, remove the core and dice finely. Mix with half of the lime juice. Add the apple and the tomatoes to the other ingredients in the pan and cook without a lid on a low heat for about 30 minutes, stirring occasionally.

Add the lime zest with the cumin, turmeric and chilli rings and boil down for 10-15 minutes until syrupy. Season with the remaining lime juice and salt. The chutney tastes good warm or cold.

Indian Beetroot Fritters

One of our best-selling dishes

Preparation time
45 minutes

Makes 8 pieces

2 large beetroots
2 medium-sized floury
potatoes
Salt
1 onion
20 g/4 tsp fresh ginger
3 small green chillies
50 g/½ cup cashews
4 sprigs fresh coriander/
cilantro
50 g/5 tbsp fresh or
frozen peas
1 tsp ground turmeric
1 tsp ground asafoetida
2 tsp ground coriander/
cilantro
2 tsp chana masala
1 tsp ground chilli
1 tsp ground cinnamon
100 g/¾ cup chickpea
flour/gram flour
Ground pepper
500 ml/2 cups oil for
frying

Peel the beetroot and potatoes, cut them into 1-cm/ half-inch pieces and cook together in salted water for 15-20 minutes until soft. Drain and leave to cool gently, then mash with a potato masher.

Peel the onion and ginger and chop finely along with the chillies, cashews and coriander/cilantro. Add the peas, vegetables and chickpea/gram flour to the beetroot-potato purée. Mix everything well and season with plenty of salt and pepper.

Shape the dough into tennis-ball-sized dumplings with damp hands and gently press flat. Fry each portion in the hot oil. Remove excess oil with kitchen paper. The beetroot fritters taste good both warm and cold.

TIPS
Chana masala is a popular Indian spice mix which, among other things, consists of coriander, cumin, pepper, chilli, pomegranate and unripe mango. Alternatively, a different mild curry mix can be used. The Indian herb asafoetida (devil's dirt), can be replaced by a finely chopped clove of garlic. The beetroot fritters go well with refreshing chutneys such as the apricot and ginger chutney (page 50) or the green tomato chutney (page 24).

Bündner Vegetable and Barley Soup

This Swiss classic really warms the soul

Preparation time
45 minutes
+ soaking time overnight

Serves 4

50 g/¼ cup white beans
(e.g. cannellini beans)
¼ leek
1 carrot
⅕ celeriac
1 tbsp neutral-flavoured
vegetable oil
80 g/½ cup pearl barley
300 ml/1¼ cups
vegetable stock
1 tsp salt
Ground white pepper
100 ml/½ cup vegan
double cream
Finely chopped chives to
garnish

Soak the beans overnight in cold water. The next day, cook them in unsalted water for at least 30 minutes until soft.

Wash and peel the vegetables and dice finely. Heat the oil and lightly fry the vegetable pieces for four minutes. Add the pearl barley and lightly fry for a further minute.

Add 500 ml/2 cups of water, the stock and the seasoning, bring to the boil and leave to simmer on a low heat covered for 30 minutes with the lid on.

Add the white beans and cook for 10 minutes. Stir in the vegan double cream and allow the soup to simmer gently without boiling. Season with salt and pepper. Serve in soup bowls and garnish with chopped chives.

TIP
If the soup is too thick, it can be
thinned with a little vegetable stock.

Roasted Almonds with Cranberries and Rosemary

Tasty appetizer or an impressive gift

Preparation time
25 minutes (including baking time)

Serves 4

2 tbsp olive oil
1 level tbsp fleur de sel
1-2 tbsp soy sauce
1 heaped tbsp raw cane sugar
100 g/½ cup blanched almonds
100 g/½ cup unblanched almonds
100 g/¾ cup cashews
1 sprig rosemary
50 g/½ cup dried cranberries

Preheat the oven to 180°C/355°F.

Mix the olive oil with the fleur de sel, soy sauce and raw cane sugar in a bowl. Add the almonds and the nuts along with the plucked rosemary needles and mix everything well.

Put the mixture on a baking tray lined with baking paper and bake in a preheated oven for 7-12 minutes. Take the tray out of the oven, add the cranberries to the warm nuts and mix everything well. Leave to cool well on the tray, then serve or store tightly sealed in a dry place.

TIPS
Raisins can also be used instead of cranberries. We recommend preparing the nuts a few hours before serving so that they have plenty of time to cool. Store the nuts in an aluminium or glass container, not in a plastic container, to stop them from going soft.

Lemongrass and Coconut Soup

A different take on a tom kha gai

Preparation time
40 minutes

Serves 4

200 g/3¼ cups oyster
mushrooms
2 tbsp neutral-flavoured
vegetable oil
6 cherry tomatoes
40 g/3 tbsp fresh
galangal
3 shallots
3 small green chillies
3 stalks lemongrass
8 kaffir lime leaves
1 litre/4¼ cups coconut
milk
800 ml/3⅓ cups
vegetable stock
Juice of 2 limes
4 tbsp soy sauce
1-2 tbsp raw cane sugar
Salt
½ bunch fresh coriander/
cilantro

Clean the oyster mushrooms and pull apart into fine strips. Heat the oil in a pan and fry the mushrooms until golden brown. Put to one side.

Wash and prepare the tomatoes and cut in half. Peel the galangal and cut into thin strips. Peel the shallots and cut into fine strips. Clean the chillies and chop finely – if you don't want it to be too spicy, remove the centres of the chillies. Bash the lemongrass stalks flat on the lower end and cut into 4-cm/1½-inch long pieces. Cut the kaffir lime leaves in half.

Bring the coconut milk and vegetable stock to the boil in a pan. Add the galangal, shallots, chillies, lemongrass and kaffir lime leaves and cook everything for 10 minutes. Season the soup with lime juice, soy sauce, raw cane sugar and salt and cook for a further 10 minutes. Remove the lemongrass shortly before serving.

Add the oyster mushrooms and the tomatoes to the soup and heat up again. Finely chop the fresh coriander/cilantro then sprinkle it on the soup and serve.

TIP
Pieces of tofu or tempeh could also be scattered on the soup.

Spiced Pineapple

Looks good, tastes good

Preparation time
25 minutes (including baking time)

1 pineapple
1 tbsp raw cane sugar
1 tsp ground turmeric
20 g/4 tsp fresh ginger
1 onion
1 clove of garlic
1 small green chilli
100 ml/7 tbsp olive oil
1 cinnamon stick
2 star anise
Salt, ground pepper

Preheat the oven to 160°C/320°F.

Peel the pineapple into 2-cm/¾-inch cubes. Mix with sugar and turmeric and arrange on a baking tray lined with baking paper. Bake the pineapple in the centre of the preheated oven for about 15 minutes.

In the meantime, peel the ginger, onion and clove of garlic and finely chop. Cut away the stalk of the chilli, cut in half lengthways, remove the centre and finely chop.

Heat the oil in a frying pan and fry the ginger, onion, garlic and chilli at a medium heat. Add 100 ml (⅓ cup plus one tbsp) water, the cinnamon stick and the star anise and simmer for 2 minutes. Fill a bowl with the sauce and leave to cool gently.

Put the warm pineapple directly from the oven into the sauce and mix well. Season with salt and pepper. Serve warm or cold.

TIPS
When preparing chillies, it is best to wear disposable kitchen gloves. This way, burns and irritations can be avoided. Filled into a preserving jar and packaged nicely, this spiced pineapple makes a great gift. It goes well with the quinoa and potato burgers (page 44) or the Indian beetroot fritters (page 27).

Kebab Sandwich

Our Turkish chefs' favourite

Preparation time
20 minutes

Makes 4 sandwiches

400 g/14 oz seitan, in one
piece
2 pinches ground
coriander
2 pinches cumin
1-2 pinches dried
oregano
1-2 pinches dried chillies
1 heaped tbsp mild
paprika
3 tbsp neutral-flavoured
vegetable oil
Salt, ground pepper
½ onion
1-2 tomatoes
½ cucumber
4 pitta or ciabatta breads
20 g/1 tbsp iceberg
lettuce leaves

Cut the seitan into thin 5-cm/2-inch long and 2-cm/¾-inch wide strips with a potato peeler. Mix well in a bowl with the herbs and spices.

Heat the oil in a frying pan and sear the seitan quickly on a high heat, turning regularly. Season with salt and pepper and put on a plate.

Peel the onion and cut into thin slices. Wash and prepare the tomato, wash the cucumber and cut both into ½-cm/⅛-inch thick slices.

Heat the bread in the oven for a few minutes and cut in half. Cover the lower half of the bread with the seitan. Put the tomato, cucumber and onion slices on top and garnish with lettuce. Put the top on the sandwich and serve.

TIP
Before adding the filling, the bread can be spread with vegan mayonnaise, cream cheese or margarine if liked, and seasoned with sambal oelek or harissa.

Carrot and Date Dip

The perfect accompaniment to fresh pitta bread

Preparation time
30 minutes

Serves 4

5 carrots
100 g/9 tbsp Medjool
dates
4 tbsp olive oil
300 ml/1¼ cups
vegetable stock
½ bunch parsley
25 g/3 tbsp pistachios
2 tsp harissa
2 pinches ground
cinnamon
Salt, ground pepper,
ground nutmeg

Peel the carrots and cut into 1-cm/⅜-inch pieces. Remove the pits from the dates and chop finely. Heat the oil in a pan and fry the carrots for 2-3 minutes. Douse with the stock, add the dates and leave everything to simmer until the carrots begin to break apart.

Meanwhile, chop the parsley and pistachios finely. Mash the carrots and the dates with a potato masher. Stir in the harissa and the cinnamon and season everything with salt, pepper and nutmeg.

Mix two-thirds of the chopped parsley and pistachios into the carrot and date mixture and sprinkle the rest over the top as garnish. Tastes good warm or cold.

TIPS
For a finer consistency, the carrots can also be puréed with a hand blender instead of with a potato masher. Harissa is a fiery, North African spice paste made from chillies and paprika. It can be bought in tubes, jars or small tins in health-food shops and supermarkets.

BLT Sandwich

The American classic with a fresh new twist

Preparation time
15 minutes

For 4 sandwiches

4 olive ciabatta rolls
(page 212)
4 tbsp rice mayonnaise
4 tbsp barbecue sauce
1 head iceberg lettuce
400 g/14 oz smoked tofu
4 small tomatoes

TIPS
Fixed with a toothpick, these mini BLTs are perfect finger food. Rice mayonnaise can be bought from health food and wholefood shops. Alternatively, homemade vegan mayonnaise can be used (page 214). The mayonnaise can be seasoned to taste, for example with fresh herbs or a little curry powder.

Cut the ciabatta rolls in half lengthways. Spread the bottom half with the rice mayonnaise and the top half with the barbecue sauce.

Wash and prepare the iceberg lettuce and shake dry. Lay 4 lettuce leaves on the upper half of each roll so that they overlap. Cut the smoked tofu into thin strips and arrange on the lower half of the bread. Wash the tomatoes, remove the stalks and cut into thin slices. Arrange the tomato slices next to each other on top of the smoked tofu.

Put the sandwich together and cut each roll into 3 pieces with a sharp knife.

Saffron Soup

A classy starter

Preparation time
50 minutes

Serves 4

2 tsp saffron threads
200 ml/¾ cup white wine
1 shallot
1 clove of garlic
½ small celeriac
1 floury potato
½ leek
2 tbsp olive oil
2 tsp raw cane sugar
1 litre/4¼ cups vegetable
stock
200 ml/¾ cup vegan
double cream
Salt, ground pepper

Soak the saffron threads in half of the white wine. Peel the shallot and clove of garlic and chop finely. Peel the celeriac and potato and cut into cubes of about 1 cm/⅜ inch. Wash and prepare the leeks and cut into fine rings.

Heat the oil in a pan and fry the shallots and clove of garlic. Add the vegetables and potato and fry for a few minutes. Sprinkle the sugar over the top and allow to caramelize. Douse with the rest of the white wine. Bring everything to the boil and reduce by half. Fill with the stock and cook for a further 20 minutes.

Add the double cream and the soaked saffron threads together with the soaking liquid to the soup and bring this to the boil again. Purée the soup finely with the hand blender and season with salt and pepper.

TIPS
For a finer consistency, pass the soup through a sieve. Fresh shoots or a milk foam are perfect garnish for this dish; for the foam, heat 100 ml (1 cup + 1 tbsp) soy milk and foam with the hand blender. The soup also tastes great with 2 tbsp popped amaranth.

Quinoa and Potato Burgers

Perfect for the whole family

Preparation time
1 hour (including baking time)

Serves 4

150 g/¾ cup each of black and white quinoa
8-9 medium-sized floury potatoes
1 large onion
2 tbsp neutral-flavoured vegetable oil
½ bunch freshly mixed herbs (thyme, parsley, rosemary, sage)
3-4 tbsp cornflour
1 level tbsp salt
1 pinch ground black pepper
1 tbsp ground madras curry powder
1 level tbsp vegetable stock powder

Boil 600 ml (2½ cups) water in a saucepan, then switch off the hob. Add the two types of quinoa, mix well and leave covered to soak for about 20 minutes, then drain the remaining water.

In the meantime, peel the potatoes, cut into 1-cm/⅜-inch cubes and boil in non-salted water until soft. Drain and allow to cool.

Peel the onion, chop finely, fry in the oil and put into a large bowl. Add the cooked quinoa grains and the diced potato. Chop the herbs finely and add to the remaining ingredients. Mix everything well until it is like a dough.

Form the mixture into burgers or balls and press flat gently. Put the burgers on a baking sheet covered with baking paper and bake in the preheated oven at 180°C/355°F for 15-20 minutes. Or fry the burgers in oil in a frying pan or deep fat fryer for 5-7 minutes. Then remove the excess oil with kitchen paper.

TIPS
The apricot and ginger chutney (page 50) goes very well with this dish. The burgers can also be cooked in advance and warmed up again in the oven at 180°C/355°F shortly before serving.

Mango Gazpacho

Our exotic version of this classic dish

Preparation time
15 minutes
+ 30 minutes cooling time

Serves 4

1 small green chilli
½ shallot
½ cucumber
500 ml/2 cups vegetable
stock
6 tbsp cider vinegar
110 g/⅓ cup ketchup
6 tbsp olive oil
250 g/9 oz mango pulp
(see tip)
Salt, ground pepper
Tabasco
½ ripe mango
1 tbsp olive oil
1 slice toasted bread
½ bunch fresh coriander/
cilantro

Cut away the stalks of the chilli and chop the chilli finely, including the seeds. Peel the shallot and roughly dice along with the cucumber. Mix everything with the vegetable stock, cider vinegar, ketchup, olive oil and mango pulp and purée with the hand blender. Season with salt, pepper and tabasco. Leave the soup to cool for at least 30 minutes.

Peel the mango, cut away the flesh of the fruit from the stone and dice finely. Heat the oil in a frying pan. Cut the toasted bread into 1-cm/½-inch cubes and fry in the hot oil until golden brown. Chop the fresh coriander/cilantro finely then sprinkle it with the diced mango and the croutons over the cooled mango gazpacho and serve.

TIPS
Jazz up the gazpacho with roasted peanuts or pine nuts, tofu pieces or wheatgerm. Mango pulp (fruit purée) can be bought in Asian food shops or supermarkets. It can also be made easily at home: for this, finely purée the flesh of one medium-sized mango with 50 ml/3 tbsp water with a hand blender and sweeten slightly with raw cane sugar.

Leek and Quinoa Soup

Warming and heartening, all in one dish

Preparation time
45 minutes

Serves 4

½ leek
1 small parsnip
2 tbsp neutral-flavoured
vegetable oil
2 floury potatoes
1 litre/4¼ cups vegetable
stock
Salt, ground pepper
50 g/¼ cup white quinoa
200 ml/¾ cup almond
milk
Finely chopped chives to
garnish

Wash and prepare the leek and cut into fine slices. Peel the parsnip and dice finely. Heat the oil in a large frying pan and fry the vegetables for 5 minutes.

Peel the potatoes and cut into 1½-cm/½-inch cubes. Add the stock, the diced potato and salt and pepper to the vegetables and leave everything to cook for about 20 minutes until the vegetables are soft.

Purée the soup with a hand blender. Add the quinoa and cook until soft. Add the almond milk and heat up. Season the soup again with salt and pepper and serve garnished with finely chopped parsley.

TIPS
Depending on your preference, fresh herbs, a little horseradish or ginger goes well with this as seasoning.

Apricot and Ginger Chutney

The winning combination of sweet and sour

Preparation time
30 minutes

Serves 4

500 g/3⅓ cups apricots
2 onions
1 red pepperoncini (mild
chilli)
20 g/4 tsp fresh ginger
125 ml/½ cup white
balsamic vinegar
150 g/¾ cup raw cane
sugar
1 tsp salt

Wash the apricots, cut in half, remove the stones and cut into 1-cm/⅜-inch cubes. Peel the onions and chop finely. Cut the pepperoncini in half, remove the centre and dice finely. Peel the ginger and again chop finely.

Purée 350 g/2⅓ cups of the diced apricot with the hand blender and put the apricot purée into a deep pan. Add the balsamic vinegar, raw cane sugar, onions, salt and the rest of the diced apricot and bring everything to the boil. As soon as the mixture is boiling, add the diced ginger and pepperoncini and boil everything down on a low heat, stirring occasionally, until the desired consistency is reached. Season with salt again, if needed, and allow the chutney to cool. The chutney can be kept in the fridge for 6 days.

TIPS
Take care when boiling down the mixture, as the chutney can quickly become too thick. The chutney goes well with the quinoa and potato burgers (page 44) or with the Indian beetroot fritters (page 27).

tibits

SALADS

Fresh, bold and surprising:
Salads which are more than
the sum of their parts

Bring back that much-needed energy: Energy and nutrient providers

There are a whole range of 'super foods' which play a fundamental part in vegan nutrition. They supply secondary plant substances, vitamins and minerals, on which the body is reliant. Here is a list of our favourite plants.

To start, there is the green brigade such as **kale, young leaf spinach, broccoli, rocket/arugula, fresh herbs and shoots, wheatgrass, green varieties of tomatoes**; they are abundant in high-quality nutrients, above all iron and calcium. They should be consumed in large quantities – and raw or prepared as carefully as possible. Ideally, the green brigade should be combined with products that are rich in vitamin C, for example berries, bell peppers or citrus fruits, to improve the uptake of minerals and micronutrients (such as iron).

The finely ground Japanese green tea **matcha** can of course be consumed as tea, but also in the form of a smoothie and is a good decoration for desserts with its striking green colour. As matcha can taste very different, we recommend being selective when choosing the right type – otherwise it could cause the food to have an unwanted bitter taste.

Different **types of seaweed** are available in health food shops and Asian food shops, such as wakame, nori or kombu. They work well with soups, salads, curries and tofu dishes, but can also be roasted and served as a crunchy topping. **Lemongrass, kaffir lime leaves and curry leaves, ginger, chillies and Asian spice mixtures** such as garam masala and five spice give many dishes that special something with their intense aromas and can transform even the simplest of meals into a taste sensation.

Kale and Swede/Rutabaga Salad

Winter in its most beautiful form

Preparation time
20 minutes

Serves 4

200 g/½ cup kale
500 g/18 oz swede/
rutabaga
40 g/⅓ cup walnuts
80 g/¾ cup dried
cranberries

For the dressing
2-3 tbsp tomato pesto
(page 210)
1-2 tbsp walnut oil
7 tbsp neutral-flavoured
vegetable oil
110 ml/8 tbsp white
balsamic vinegar
Salt, ground pepper

Clean and prepare the kale and cut into 1cm thick strips. Blanch in boiling water for 3-4 minutes, then drain and allow to dry well before putting in a bowl.

Peel the swede/rutabaga, cut into thin slices, cut in half or quarters depending on size and cook in boiling water for 5 minutes. Drain, leave to dry well and add to the kale. Add the walnuts and the cranberries to the vegetables and mix.

Mix the ingredients for the dressing well. Season with salt and pepper. Add to the vegetables, mixing everything well and serve.

TIPS
The salad can be garnished, for example, with beetroot sprouts, red basil or borage flowers. Kale is rich in vitamin C and is very healthy.

Asian Glass Noodle Salad

A light and crunchy summer dish for sweet and sour fans

Preparation time
20 minutes

Serves 4

200 g/2¼ cups fine glass
noodles
Salt
1 carrot
1 spring onion/scallion
½ of each of a red and
yellow bell pepper
1 head of celery

For the dressing
80 ml/⅓ cup sweet chilli
sauce
60 ml/4 tbsp freshly
squeezed lemon juice
3 tbsp soy sauce
1 pinch salt
1 pinch ground white
pepper

Cook the glass noodles in boiling salted water for 2 minutes. Cool immediately under cold running water and allow to drain well. Then cut into pieces 5 cm/2 inches long.

Peel the carrots and slice into fine strips on the vegetable grater. Wash and prepare the spring onion/scallion and cut into fine strips. Cut the bell peppers in half, remove the centre, wash and cut into thin pieces. Wash and prepare the celery, cut in half lengthways and again cut into tiny ½-cm/⅛-inch cubes.

For the dressing, mix the sweet chilli sauce with the lemon juice and the soy sauce and season with salt and pepper. Add the vegetables and the dressing to the noodles, mix well and leave to infuse for a few minutes.

TIP
Add freshly picked coriander/
cilantro and a little ground
ginger, if liked, for an authentic
Asian touch.

Quinoa
Tomaten
Frühlingszwiebeln
Peperoni
Limette
Pfefferminze

Peruvian Quinoa Salad

A taste of Peru, refreshing and lively

Preparation time
35 minutes

Serves 4

1 level tsp salt
125 g/½ cup white
quinoa
2 spring onions/scallions
1 sprig of mint
1 tomato
½ red or yellow bell
pepper

For the dressing
Juice of 2 limes
1 tbsp chilli oil
3 tbsp olive oil
1 level tsp salt

Boil 1 litre/4 cups water, add the salt and the quinoa. Leave to simmer on a low heat for about 20 minutes. Drain using a fine sieve and allow to cool.

Wash the spring onions/scallions and the mint and shake dry. Cut both into fine strips. Wash the tomato, remove the stalk and cut into ½-cm/⅛-inch pieces. Cut the pepper in half, remove the centre, wash and cut into ½cm pieces. Add all of the vegetables and the mint to the cooled quinoa.

Mix all of the ingredients for the dressing, drizzle over the salad and mix well.

TIP
Garnish with a slice of lime.

Thai Papaya Salad

Perfect for a taste of Thailand

Preparation time
30 minutes
+ 20 minutes infusion
time

Serves 4

For the dressing
2 small green chillies
1 clove of garlic
2 limes
100 ml/7 tbsp soy sauce
60 g/5 tbsp palm sugar

For the salad
1 small, unripe, green
papaya
2 carrots
100 g/½ cup yardlong
beans
4 cherry tomatoes
Salt, ground pepper
80 g/½ cup peanuts

For the dressing, cut away the stalks of the chilli and finely chop. Peel the garlic and again finely chop. Squeeze the limes; they should produce 50 ml/3 tbsp of juice. Add the garlic and chillies with the lime juice, soy sauce and palm sugar to a pan and heat gently until the sugar has melted. Remove from the hob and allow to cool.

For the salad, peel the papaya, cut in half, remove the seeds and slice or grate the zest of the fruit into very fine strips with a julienne cutter or a potato peeler. Peel the carrots and again slice into fine strips. Alternatively, cut the papaya and the carrots lengthways into ½-cm/¼-inch thick slices and cut these slices into fine, thin strips.

Prepare the yardlong beans, cut off the end pieces and cut the beans across into 2-cm/¾-inch pieces. Wash the cherry tomatoes, remove the stalks and cut in half lengthways. Mix the ingredients for the salad together in a bowl.

Add the dressing to the salad, carefully mix all the way through and season with salt and pepper. Leave to infuse for at least 20 minutes. Shortly before serving, roughly chop the peanuts and sprinkle them over the salad.

TIPS
An unripe, green papaya is needed for this salad and not the ripened yellow-orange fruit. Unripe, green papayas can be bought in Asian food shops. To reduce the spice, remove the seeds of the chillies along with the white inner pith, which is also very spicy.

Black Salsify and Kumquat Salad

A wonderful winter salad

Preparation time
30 minutes

Serves 4

700 g/25 oz black salsify
100 g/3½ oz kumquats
1 tsp white sugar

For the dressing:
4 tbsp rice or almond
mayonnaise
1-2 tbsp orange syrup
60 g/¼ cup vegan cream
cheese
Salt, ground black
pepper
1-2 pinches black
caraway seeds to garnish

Wash and peel the black salsify under cold running water (protect your hands with kitchen paper as this can leave stubborn stains). As you go, place the peeled salsify in cold water. Then cut the black salsify into 3-cm/1¼-inch long pieces and cook in boiling water for 7-9 minutes. Drain, rinse and allow to drain well before putting in a bowl.

Cut the kumquats into very thin strips, boil down with 50 ml/3 tbsp water and the sugar, allow to cool and then put to one side.

Put the ingredients for the dressing in a bowl, mix well and add to the black salsify together with the kumquats. Mix everything well, plate up and garnish with the black caraway seeds.

TIP
Instead of the kumquats, a small peeled orange that is cut into strips is also suitable. Instead of the orange syrup, fresh orange juice and a little sugar can also be used. However, the sauce will then be thinner.

Apple and Lentil Salad

Beluga lentils with a hint of sweetness

Preparation time
40 minutes

Serves 4

300 g/1½ cups Beluga
lentils
2 medium-sized apples
60 g/¼ cup raw cane
sugar
150 ml/⅔ cup cider
vinegar
1 bunch parsley
150 ml/9 tbsp neutral-
flavoured vegetable oil
1 pinch chilli powder
Salt, ground pepper

Sort through the lentils (there could be small stones mixed in) and rinse thoroughly. Simmer in boiling, unsalted water for about 30 minutes until soft. Drain and leave to dry.

In the meantime, peel the apples, remove the cores and dice finely. Heat the sugar together with the vinegar until the sugar has dissolved. Add the diced apple and allow the liquid to cool.

Finely chop the parsley. When the liquid is lukewarm, mix in the finely chopped parsley, oil and chilli powder. Pour the sauce over the still-warm lentils and season with salt and pepper. Serve hot or cold.

TIPS
For a crunchier texture, use apple with the peel still on. If the lentils are cooked for too long, they will fall apart and will not look as good – so test them every once in a while.

Cassava and Pineapple Salad

An exotic treat

Preparation time
30 minutes

Serves 4

½ small cassava
1 shallot
3 tbsp olive oil
2 pinches ground saffron
1 tsp mild paprika
1 tsp ground coriander
1 tsp ground cumin
3 tsp lemon juice
1 small pineapple
Salt, ground pepper
3 sprigs parsley

Peel the cassava, cut into quarters lengthways, cut out the hard inner core and cut the cassava into 2-cm/¾-inch cubes. Cook in boiling, salted water for about 20 minutes until soft and then drain.

In the meantime, peel the shallot and chop finely. Heat the oil in a frying pan and glaze the diced shallot in this. Mix in 100 ml/1 cup + 1 tbsp water, the spices and the lemon juice. Remove from the hob and allow to cool.

Mix the dressing with the still hot cassava pieces and allow to cool.

Peel the pineapple, cut into 2-cm/¾-inch cubes. Mix the pineapple with the cooled cassava pieces and season everything with salt and pepper. Finely chop the parsley. Scatter the parsley over the salad and serve.

TIP
For that special something,
scatter the salad with a handful of
roasted, roughly chopped walnuts
or 1 tbsp roasted chia seeds.

Beetroot and Apple Salad

Bright red, crunchy, delicious

Preparation time
30 minutes
+ 30 minutes infusion
time

Serves 4

5 beetroots
100 ml/7 tbsp orange
juice
2 apples

For the dressing
20 g/4 tsp fresh ginger
50 ml/3 tbsp white
balsamic vinegar
1 tsp harissa
150 ml/⅔ cup neutral-
flavoured vegetable oil
Salt, ground pepper

Peel the beetroots and grate into fine strips with a julienne cutter or a grater. Mix the beetroots in a bowl with the orange juice. Wash the apples, cut into quarters and remove the cores. Grate into the bowl with the beetroots and mix well.

For the dressing, peel the ginger and chop finely. Put this into a tall container together with the other ingredients for the dressing and mix into a smooth sauce with the hand blender. Season with salt and pepper.

Pour the dressing over the grated apple and beetroot, mix together and leave everything to infuse for at least 30 minutes.

TIPS
As the beetroots have a strong colour, it is best to wear disposable gloves during preparation. Instead of apple, this salad also tastes great with pears. For an additional kick of colour and freshness, mix in half a bunch of chopped parsley.

Okra Antipasto

An Indian appetizer

Preparation time
30 minutes
+ 20 minutes infusion
time

Serves 4

700 g/25 oz okra
500 ml/2 cups oil for
frying
5 cloves of garlic
2 tbsp olive oil
4 medium-sized
tomatoes
½ bunch fresh coriander/
cilantro
1 unwaxed lemon
1 tsp raw cane sugar
Salt

Cut away the stalks of the okra, cut them in half and deep-fry in portions in hot oil until golden brown. Remove the excess oil with kitchen paper.

Peel the cloves of garlic and slice finely. Heat the olive oil in a frying pan and gently fry the garlic on a low heat – do not allow it to burn or it will taste bitter!

Wash the tomatoes, remove the stalks and cut the flesh into 2-cm/¾-inch pieces. Mix the tomatoes with the okra and mix with the seared garlic.

Finely chop the fresh coriander/cilantro. Wash the lemon with hot water, dry and grate the zest with a zester or a fine grater; squeeze the juice. Add the lemon zest, 1 tsp lemon juice, the finely chopped coriander/cilantro and the sugar to the okra, mix together and season with salt. Leave to infuse for at least 20 minutes.

TIPS
Instead of deep-frying, the okra can also be fried in portions in hot oil in a frying pan. They go well both with Mediterranean dishes such as parsnip gnocchi (page 116) or spelt risotto with tomatoes (page 119), and with Asian dishes such as dal pancharangi (page 126) or aloo bhaji (page 131).

Asparagus and Mango Salad

An unusual but delightful combination

Preparation time
45 minutes

Serves 4

1 kg/35 oz white
asparagus
800 g/28 oz green
asparagus
Salt
1 tbsp raw cane sugar
2 ripe mangos
2 spring onions/scallions
100 g/¼ cup rocket/
arugula

For the dressing
10 g/2 tsp fresh ginger
4 tbsp white balsamic
dressing
70 ml/5 tbsp orange juice
70 g/2½ oz mango pulp
(see tip page 47)
70 ml/¼ cup neutral-
flavoured vegetable oil
1 tsp sambal oelek
Salt, ground pepper

Snap off the woody end of the two types of asparagus. Peel the white asparagus carefully with a potato peeler and cut into 2.5-cm/1-inch pieces. Only peel the lower third of the green asparagus, and again cut into 2.5-cm/1-inch pieces. Put the asparagus tips to one side. Cook the asparagus pieces in boiling, salted water with the sugar for about 5 minutes until crisp. Shortly before the end of the cooking time, add the asparagus tips for 1 minute. Drain and leave to dry.

Peel the mangos, cut the flesh from the stone and cut into 1½-cm/½-inch pieces. Wash the spring onions/ scallions, prepare and cut into rings. Remove the tough stalks from the rocket/arugula, carefully wash and shake dry.

For the dressing, peel the ginger and dice finely. Put in a high container together with the other ingredients and purée with the hand blender. Season with salt and pepper.

Carefully mix the rocket/arugula, asparagus and mango in a bowl with the dressing. Scatter the chopped spring onions/scallions over the salad and serve.

TIPS
2 tbsp roasted hemp or sesame seeds can be scattered over the salad as a crunchy garnish. Sambal oelek is an Indonesian chilli paste made from fresh red chillies, salt and brown sugar. Alternatively, half a small red chilli can be used or 1 pinch chilli powder.

Squash Salad with Sesame Seeds

A feast for the eyes and palate

Preparation time
30 minutes (including
baking time)

Serves 4

1.6 kg/56 oz butternut
squash
2 tbsp sesame seeds for
sprinkling

For the dressing:
3 tbsp walnut oil
3 tbsp white balsamic
vinegar
1 tsp vegetable stock
powder
1 pinch ground white
pepper
½ tsp chilli oil
½ tsp salt

Preheat fan oven to 200°C/390°F.

Peel the squash, remove the core and the white fibres
and cut the flesh into 1½-cm/½-inch cubes. Spread
the diced squash evenly over a baking try lined with
baking paper and bake in the oven for 8-10 minutes.
The pieces should not be too soft. Leave to cool on the
baking tray.

Mix the ingredients for the dressing. Pour the dressing
over the still-warm diced squash and mix carefully.
Serve in a dish or bowl and scatter with sesame seeds
on top.

TIP
The salad tastes best when still warm.

Chirashi Sushi

Traditional 'open sushi' from Japan

Preparation time
40 minutes

Serves 4

50 g/3 tbsp canned
bamboo shoots
2 carrots
100 g/1½ cup shiitake
mushrooms
150 g fresh or frozen soy
beans
100 g/6 tbsp bean
sprouts
250 g/1¼ cup sushi rice
150 ml/⅔ cup rice wine
vinegar
A few strips of kizami
nori seaweed
1 tsp roasted sesame
seeds

Drain the bamboo shoots and rinse well. Peel the carrots and cut into fine strips, together with the bamboo shoots. Wash and prepare the shiitake mushrooms and again cut into fine strips. Mix with the bean sprouts and the soy beans.

Wash the sushi rice thoroughly until the water runs clear. Then bring to the boil in 350 ml/1½ cups fresh cold water, mix well and leave to simmer on a low heat for 10 minutes with the lid on. Remove the pan from the hob and leave the rice to infuse for 15 minutes with the lid on, so that all of the liquid has been absorbed.

In the meantime, steam the prepared vegetables for 4 minutes. Add the lukewarm vegetables to the rice and mix. Add the rice wine vinegar to the rice and vegetable mixture and allow the salad to cool. Before plating up, mix in the strips of seaweed and garnish with sesame seeds.

TIPS
Sushi ginger and wasabi go well with this. Peas can also be used instead of the soya beans. If the sushi is prepared in advance, add a little rice wine vinegar and mix in before serving.

Crunchy Detox Salad with Lemon Dressing

For fans of raw vegetables: crunchy and light

Preparation time
30 minutes

Serves 4

1 carrot
1 yellow carrot
¼ radish
1 stick celery
1 bunch of each of
chervil and tarragon
30 g/2 tbsp sunflower
sprouts
30 g/2 tbsp radish,
beetroot and onion
sprouts, mixed

For the dressing
2 tbsp freshly squeezed
lemon juice
3 tbsp cold-pressed olive
oil
Salt, ground pepper

Prepare and peel or wash the vegetables. Cut the carrots and the radish into fine sticks of about 5 cm/2 inches in length; cut the celery into 1-cm/⅜-inch thick slices. Wash the herbs and pluck into small pieces. Add the sprouts and the herbs to the vegetables and mix well.

Mix the ingredients for the dressing; season with salt and pepper. Plate up the salad, sprinkle with the dressing and serve.

TIPS
Depending on the season, watercress, edible flowers, beetroot and broccoli leaves go well in this mixture. The salad also tastes good without the dressing.

Hiltl

Hiltl

HOT DISHES

Diverse, hearty and delicious:
Main courses from
around the world

The muscle factor: soy and seitan, our protein providers

Countless nutrient-rich dishes can be made from the soy bean. However, it is important to consider the quality of the cultivated soy bean when shopping. Organic production generally means sustainable cultivation and guarantees that you are not putting a genetically altered food product on the table.

Soy beans contain high-quality protein and are rich in vitamins, minerals and specific secondary plant substances which are important for the functioning of the human body. Possibly the most well-known product produced from soy beans is tofu, which has a protein proportion of about 10 per cent. **Tofu** has a mild, delicate taste. It can be bought in 'pure' or smoked form, goes well with all types of seasonings and can therefore be used in many different ways: fried and marinated, raw and in sauces or prepared as a filling. A correspondingly large range of prepared tofu dishes are available on the market.

A particularly fine variety of tofu is so-called **silken tofu**. This has the consistency of set yoghurt and is great in desserts, dips, salad dressings, sauces or cake fillings.

The Indonesian speciality **tempeh** is made from fermented soya beans. It has a fine, nutty taste and can be bought in 'pure' and smoked form. Creamy dressings and spreads can be made from steamed and puréed tempeh. Minced and roasted tempeh is an excellent garnish for salads or Asian dishes. What is more, tempeh is the soy product that has the highest vitamin B12 content of all vegan products, as well as having excellent nutritional value with 19-per-cent protein.

Fermented soy beans are also the base for Japanese **miso pastes** which, as well as many vitamins and minerals, also contain useful enzymes and lactic acid bacteria, and which provide many dishes with a Far Eastern, spicy note with their powerful aromas. Additionally, miso pastes have a slight binding effect. It is important that the spice pastes are not cooked with the other ingredients but are added at the end of the cooking process – otherwise the useful components evaporate.

During soy milk production, a crumbly pulp by the name of **okara** is produced, which contains many of the useful ingredients of the soy bean. It can be used with excellent results in dumplings, rissoles, burgers and cakes – however, it can only be bought from selected shops.

Textured soy protein, on the other hand, is very common. It can be bought in the form of mince, fillets, escalopes or in small pieces. Most of the time, soy protein is already seasoned and is pre-prepared. With it, you can easily create vegan versions of spaghetti bolognese, chilli con carne or lasagne.

An alternative to soy products is **seitan**, which is pure wheat protein. Seitan was discovered by Buddhist monks and has a very similar consistency to meat. Those who don't want to miss out on dishes such as escalopes, kebabs, roasts, schnitzel or roulades have an ideal starting product with seitan to enjoy vegan versions of these dishes, and it contains a noteworthy 15 to 20 per cent protein. Seitan can be bought from wholefood shops marinated, seasoned, and in dumpling or escalope form, produced both from wheat and from spelt. You can also buy ready-made seitan powder (wheat gluten) if you would prefer to make it yourself: the powder simply needs to be mixed with water and seasonings. Seitan is an essential component of Buddhist cuisine and is popular all over East and South Asia.

Kashmir Fruit Curry

Exotic, fruity: a crowd pleaser

Preparation time
40 minutes

Serves 4

2 small green chillies
3 onions
20 g/4 tsp fresh ginger
2 tbsp neutral-flavoured
vegetable oil
½ tsp ground cardamom
1 tsp ground turmeric
1 tsp ground coriander
1 tsp ground cumin
½ tsp garam masala
1 tbsp raw cane sugar
1 tbsp desiccated coconut
1 sprig fresh coriander/
cilantro
320 ml/1⅓ cup coconut
milk
100 ml/7 tbsp vegetable
stock
½ pineapple
1 medium-sized papaya
3 medium-sized apples
2 tbsp cashews
Salt, ground pepper

Cut away the stalks of the chillies and chop finely. Peel the onions and ginger and again chop finely.

Heat the oil in a pan, add the onions, ginger and chillies and fry on a medium heat. Add the spices, the sugar, the desiccated coconut and the fresh coriander/cilantro and fry with the other ingredients. Fill the pan with coconut milk and stock and cook for about 20 minutes.

Peel the pineapple and cut into 2-cm/¾-inch cubes. Peel the papaya, cut in half, remove the core and cut the fruit flesh into 2-cm/¾-inch pieces. Wash the apples, remove the cores and cut into 2-cm/¾-inch pieces. Dry roast the cashews in a small frying pan.

Add the pineapple and apples to the curry, heat up again and season with salt and pepper. Shortly before serving, add the diced papaya and serve the curry with the roasted cashews sprinkled on top.

TIPS
Garam masala is the most commonly used spice mix in north India, consisting, among other things, of cinnamon, cloves, black pepper, cardamom, cumin and nutmeg. Alternatively, another intense-tasting curry mix can be used. Garnish the curry with freshly chopped herbs and pomegranate seeds and, if liked, combine with rice and refreshing dips such as, for example, the carrot and date dip (page 38).

Mushroom, Potato and Ale Pie

Inspired by a British classic

Preparation time
55 minutes (including baking time)

Makes 1 pie, serves 4

200 g/2½ cups large white mushrooms
400 g/5¼ cups mixed mushrooms (depending on the season, porcini mushrooms, oyster mushrooms, shiitake, chanterelles, etc)
2 waxy potatoes
1 large onion
1 clove of garlic
1 stick of celery
2-3 sprigs fresh thyme
2 tbsp neutral-flavoured vegetable oil
20 g/4 tsp soy margarine
1-2 level tbsp cornflour/ cornstarch
40 g/3 tbsp dark miso paste
1-2 level tbsp vegetable stock powder
1 pinch salt
1 pinch ground white pepper
250ml/1 cup ale
250 g/8½ oz vegan puff pastry
Neutral-flavoured vegetable oil for brushing

Prepare the mushrooms, wipe with a damp cloth or wash and cut into 1½-cm/½-inch pieces. Peel the potatoes and cut into 1-cm/¾-inch pieces. Peel the onions and the garlic, wash and prepare the celery and dice everything finely. Pluck the thyme leaves.

Heat the oil and the margarine in a frying pan. Fry the potato and celery cubes with the onions and the garlic for 4 minutes. Add the mushrooms and the thyme leaves and fry for a further 5 minutes.

Dissolve the cornflour/cornstarch, miso paste, vegetable stock powder and seasoning in the ale and add to the mushrooms. Leave to simmer for a further 10 minutes and season with salt and pepper. Pour into an oven-proof tin and allow to cool.

Preheat the oven to 180°C/355°F.

Roll out the puff pastry and prick finely with a fork so that it rises evenly when baking. Cover the tin with the pastry. Brush the pastry with oil and bake the pie in the oven at 180°C/355°F for 25-35 minutes.

TIP
Ale is better for this recipe than lager types of beer.

Courgette/Zucchini Schnitzel

A treat even for 'big kids'!

Preparation time
40 minutes

Serves 4 (approx 12 schnitzels)

2 large courgettes/
zucchini
Salt
40 g/¼ cup sesame seeds
80 g/1¼ cup vegan
breadcrumbs
7 tbsp soy milk
2½ tbsp cornflour/
cornstarch
Ground pepper
80 g/9 tbsp white flour

TIPS
Take care that the schnitzels are not lying on top of one another when kept warm in the oven, as they will become soft. For more variety, add oats or wheatgerm to the breadcrumbs. The pickled star fruit (page 21) and the chicory and orange bake (page 99) taste great with these.

Wash and prepare the courgettes/zucchini and cut into thin slices. Sprinkle the slices with a little salt and leave to infuse for 10 minutes, until water escapes from them. Pat dry with kitchen paper.

Preheat the oven to 60°C/140°F.

Dry roast the sesame seeds in a small frying pan. Then mix with the breadcrumbs on a deep plate. Prepare two further deep plates: on one, mix the soy milk with the cornflour/cornstarch and season well with salt and pepper. Put the flour on the other plate.

First coat the dried courgette/zucchini slices in the flour, then carefully dip in the soy milk and cornflour/cornstarch mixture and finally turn a few times in the sesame seed and breadcrumb mixture. Take care that the courgette/zucchini slices are completely covered with each ingredient; you will possibly need to dip them in the soy mixture again and then turn in the breadcrumbs. Press the breadcrumbs on with your fingers.

Heat half of the oil in a pan and, immediately after covering them in breadcrumbs, fry the schnitzel in portions on both sides until golden brown – do not let the oil get too hot or the sesame seeds will burn. Lay the finished schnitzels next to one another on a baking tray lined with baking paper and keep warm in the centre of the preheated oven. After half of the schnitzels are complete, heat the remaining oil in the pan and fry the rest of the schnitzels.

Cut the lemon into slices and garnish the schnitzels with 1 lemon slice each. They taste good hot or cold.

Lentil Stew

For cold winter days

Preparation time
45 minutes

Serves 4

500 g/2½ cups puy
lentils
2 medium-sized pears
2 onions
4 tbsp olive oil
1 sprig rosemary
300 ml/1¼ cups vegan
red wine
300 ml/1¼ cups cloudy
apple cider
100 g/9 tbsp raisins
1 pinch chilli powder
Salt, ground pepper
200 g/7 oz smoked tofu

Carefully sort through the lentils (sometimes small stones can be mixed in) and rinse thoroughly. Cook in boiling, unsalted water for 25-30 minutes until soft. Drain and leave to dry.

In the meantime, wash the pears, remove the cores and cut into about 1½-cm/½-inch pieces or thin slices. Heat 2 tbsp oil in a pan and glaze the onions. Add the pears and the rosemary sprigs and fry together for a few minutes. Cover with red wine and apple cider. Add the raisins and the chilli powder and season everything with salt and pepper. Leave to boil for about 10 minutes on a medium heat.

Cut the smoked tofu into 1x2-cm/½x¾-inch pieces. Heat 2 tbsp oil and fry the smoked tofu until golden brown. Remove excess oil with kitchen paper.

When the pears are almost ready, add the lentils and bring to the boil for a few minutes. Season with salt and pepper. Serve the lentil stew with the smoked tofu scattered on top.

TIPS
French puy lentils are not floury and therefore are not as soft as other types of lentils when cooked. Because they are very small and do not have to be soaked, they are excellent for quick meals. Alternatively, beluga lentils can be used. The stew goes well with light salads made from root vegetables such as the kale and swede/rutabaga salad (page 59) or the black salsify and kumquat salad (page 66).

Chicory and Orange Bake

Smoky and earthy, not at all bitter

Preparation time
30 minutes (including
baking time)

Serves 4

400 g/14 oz white
chicory
2 oranges

For the sauce:
8 g/1½ tsp fresh ginger
2 tbsp raw cane sugar
2 tbsp dark balsamic
vinegar
4 tbsp neutral-flavoured
vegetable oil
1-2 level tsp smoked salt

Preheat the oven to 180°C/355°F.

Cut away the ends of the chicory. If the chicory is very large, cut this in half lengthways or even into quarters. Blanch the chicory in boiling water for 2-3 minutes. Drain, allow to dry well and put into an oven dish. Peel the oranges, cut in half and then into 3mm/⅛-inch thick pieces and lay evenly on top of the chicory.

Peel the ginger, chop and mix well with the rest of the ingredients for the sauce. Pour the sauce evenly over the chicory and the oranges and bake everything in the oven for 10-15 minutes.

TIP
The dish can be prepared a day in advance; the following day simply pour over the sauce and bake.

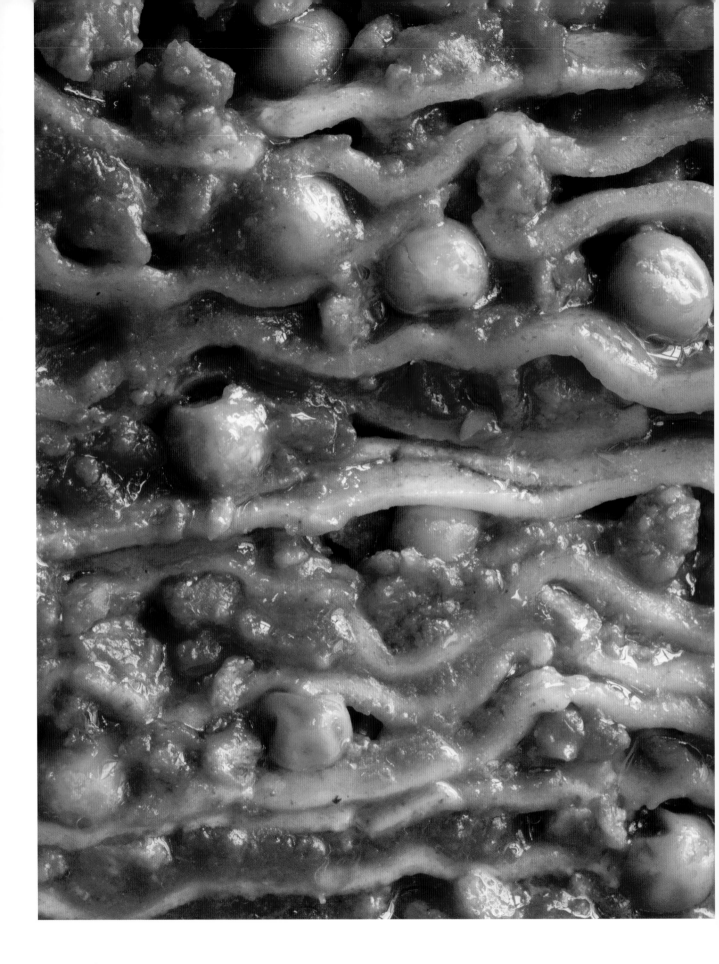

Lasagne Bolognese

The Italian classic

Preparation time
1 hour 20 minutes
(including baking time)

Serves 4

4-5 tomatoes
1 large carrot
1 large onion
1 red bell pepper
4 tbsp neutral-flavoured
vegetable oil
500 g/18 oz fresh soy
mince
1-2 tbsp ground paprika
70 ml/5 tbsp red wine
300 ml/1¼ cup vegetable
stock
1 tsp chilli oil
200 g/1¼ cup peas
1-2 tsp salt
1 pinch ground pepper
300 g lasagne sheets
2 level tbsp nutritional
yeast flakes

Remove the stalks from the tomatoes, cut a cross into the bottom and cover with boiling water. Remove the skins, cut into quarters and remove the cores. Finely dice the fruit flesh.

Peel the carrot and the onion, cut the bell pepper in half, remove the centre and wash. Dice everything finely.

Heat the oil in a wide pan and fry the diced vegetable, add the soy mince, dust with the ground paprika and fry for a few minutes. Douse with red wine and leave to boil down a little. Add the stock, the chilli oil and the tomato pieces and bring everything to the boil. Add the peas and boil everything down until you get a smooth sauce. Season with salt and pepper.

Preheat the oven to 180°C/355°F.

Layer the lasagne sheets and the sauce alternately in an oven-proof dish and finish with a layer of sauce. Sprinkle the lasagne with the yeast and bake in the oven for 40 minutes.

TIP
Dried soy mince can also be used
instead of fresh.

Tomato and Tofu Sambal

Indonesia sends its regards

Preparation time
40 minutes

Serves 4

For the sambal
2 tomatoes
2 cloves of garlic
2 tbsp neutral-flavoured
vegetable oil
4 tsp soy sauce
1 squeeze lemon juice
2 tsp raw cane sugar
2 tsp tomato purée/paste
1 pinch ground chilli
Salt, ground pepper

For the tofu
400 g/14 oz deep-fried
tofu
2 tbsp neutral-flavoured
vegetable oil
½ bunch fresh coriander/
cilantro

For the sambal, remove the stalks from the tomatoes, cut a cross into the bottom and cover with boiling water, then remove the skin, cut into quarters, remove the cores and finely dice. Peel the garlic and chop finely.

Heat the oil in a frying pan and carefully fry the garlic on a medium heat – do not allow the garlic to burn or it will become bitter. Add the tomatoes and fry for 2 minutes. Add 8 tbsp water, the soy sauce, the lemon juice, the sugar and the tomato purée/paste, bring to the boil and simmer on a low heat for 5 minutes. Add the chilli powder and season everything with salt and pepper.

Cut the deep-fried tofu into 2-cm/¾-inch thick pieces. Heat the oil in a pan and fry the tofu pieces for a few minutes on both sides until golden brown. Chop the fresh coriander/cilantro finely. Drizzle the tomato sambal over the tofu slices and sprinkle with the finely chopped coriander/cilantro.

TIPS
Deep-fried tofu can be bought from Asian food shops. If necessary, it can be replaced with normal tofu. Press this flat overnight between two plates and with a weight to achieve a firmer consistency. Pat dry with kitchen paper, cut into strips and deep-fry until golden brown. The tofu goes well with the Asian glass noodle salad (page 60) or the okra antipasto (page 75). Jasmine rice could also be served with the latter.

Caramelized Vegetables with Figs and Pears

A surprisingly good combination

Preparation time
40 minutes (including baking time)

For 1 baking tray, enough for 4 portions

200 g/1¼ cup dried figs
4-5 shallots
200 g/2½ cups white or brown mushrooms
5 carrots
3-4 pears, as hard as possible
1-2 level tbsp salt
5 tbsp olive oil
3 tbsp white balsamic vinegar

Cook the figs in boiling water for 1 minute, then drain and allow to cool. Cut the figs into quarters and place in a large bowl. Peel the shallots, prepare the mushrooms and clean with a damp cloth. Cut the shallots and mushrooms into halves or quarters depending on the size and add to the figs.

Peel the carrots and cut into 4-cm/1½-inch long pieces, cut these lengthways into ½-cm/⅛-inch thick strips and add to the prepared ingredients. Wash the pears, cut into quarters, remove the cores, cut into 2-cm/¾-inch thick pieces and add to the fig and vegetable mixture.

Preheat the oven to 180°C/355°F.

Add the salt, olive oil and balsamic vinegar, mix everything well and place on a baking tray lined with baking paper. Bake in a preheated oven for 15-20 minutes.

TIP
If liked, fresh herbs can be added to the recipe, for example rosemary or thyme.

Lahmacun

Our vegan Turkish pizza

Preparation time
1 hour 20 minutes,
including time to rise
and baking time

Makes 1 baking tray,
enough for 6 portions

For the dough
400 g/3 cups white flour
1 level tsp salt
20 g/2 tbsp fresh yeast
½ tsp sugar
3 tbsp olive oil

For the topping
2 small onions
1 clove of garlic
½ bunch parsley
2 tomatoes
250 g/9 oz fresh soy
mince
1 tbsp sambal oelek
1 pinch mild ground
paprika
2-3 tbsp tomato purée/
paste
5 tbsp neutral-flavoured
vegetable oil
1 level tbsp salt
Ground black pepper

For the dough, mix the flour with the salt and form a hollow in the centre. Mix the yeast with 50 ml/3½ tbsp lukewarm water and the sugar and pour into the hollow, mixing with a little flour from the edge. Leave for 15 minutes in a warm place.

Then add 150ml/⅔ cup warm water and the oil and thoroughly knead everything into a dough. Leave covered for a further 30-40 minutes.

Preheat the oven to 180°C/355°F.

For the topping, peel the onions and the garlic and finely chop. Finely chop the parsley. Wash the tomatoes, remove the stalks, cut into ½-cm/⅛-inch cubes. Add the onions, garlic, soy mince and the remaining ingredients to the diced tomato and mix everything well. Season with pepper to taste.

Roll the dough out thinly and lay on a baking tray lined with baking paper; stick with a fork. Cover the base evenly with the topping and bake in the preheated oven for 20-25 minutes.

TIPS
Instead of fresh soy mince, dried can also be used. This needs to be soaked in advance. If you have only a little time, buy a ready-made flat bread.

Potato and Chestnut stew with Spätzle

A hearty autumn dish

Preparation time
30 minutes
+ 30 minutes for the
spätzle

Serves 4

4-5 waxy potatoes
2 tomatoes
1 large onion
2 tbsp neutral-flavoured
vegetable oil
3 tbsp ground paprika
50 ml/3 tbsp red wine
600 ml/2½ cups
vegetable stock
200 g/7 oz frozen, peeled
chestnuts
Salt, ground pepper
1 kg homemade spätzle
(page 208)

Peel the potatoes and cut into 2½-cm/1-inch cubes. Wash the tomatoes, remove the stalks, and cut a cross on the bottom. Cover with boiling water, remove the skin, cut into quarters and remove the cores. Dice the fruit flesh finely.

Peel the onion and dice. Heat the oil in a deep pan; fry the onion pieces until golden brown. Add the ground paprika and fry gently. Douse with red wine and bring to the boil. Add the vegetable stock and bring to the boil again, add the chestnuts and the potato pieces and leave to cook on a low heat. The potatoes may still have a slight crunch.

Finally, add the pieces of tomato and bring to the boil once more. Season with salt and pepper and serve on a plate together with the homemade spätzle.

TIPS
Do not fry the paprika powder on too high a temperature or it will become bitter! As an alternative to the spätzle, the homemade mashed potato (page 209) also goes well with this dish.

Cottage Pie

Comfort food at its best

Preparation time:
1 hour (including baking time)
+ 30 minutes for the mashed potato

Serves 4

1 onion
1 small clove of garlic
1 carrot
⅕ celeriac
800 g/5 cups tomatoes
3 tbsp neutral-flavoured vegetable oil
100 ml/7 tbsp red wine
2 sprigs fresh thyme
1-2 tsp salt
1 pinch ground pepper
1 bay leaf
150 g/5 oz dried soy mince
1kg/4¾ cups mashed potatoes (page 209)

Peel the onion and finely chop. Peel the garlic and crush. Peel the carrots and celeriac and dice finely. Wash the tomatoes, remove the stalks and dice finely.

Heat the oil, add the onions and the garlic and glaze for 2 minutes. Add the carrots and the celeriac pieces and fry for a further 3 minutes. Douse with the red wine. Add the tomato pieces, 500 ml/2 cups water, the sprigs of thyme and the vegetables. Leave to boil down at a medium heat for 15 minutes.

Add the soy mince, boil for a few minutes and leave to infuse for 30 minutes. In this time, make the mashed potatoes (see page 209).

Preheat the oven to 180°C/355°F.

Remove the sprigs of thyme and the bay leaf from the sauce. Fill an oven-proof dish with the soy mince and sauce mixture. Cover with the mashed potato. Before baking, draw fine stripes in the potato purée, so that it browns up nicely. Bake in the oven for 25-30 minutes.

TIPS
If you would like to use fresh soy mince, this can be fried and then added to the sauce.

Mango and Banana Curry

Pure joie de vivre

Preparation time:
30 minutes

Serves 4

300 g/10 oz cassava
1 onion
1 bell pepper
1 red pepperoncini (mild
chilli)
2 mangos
2 bananas
5 tbsp neutral-flavoured
vegetable oil
1 pinch crushed
coriander seeds
8 fresh curry leaves
400 ml/1⅔ cups vegan
double cream
1 tbsp lemon juice
3 tbsp soy sauce
Salt, ground pepper

Peel the cassava and cut into 1½-cm/½-inch cubes. Cook in boiling water for 4 minutes, then drain and allow to cool on a plate.

Peel the onion, cut in half and cut into very thin slices. Cut the bell pepper in half, remove the centre, wash and cut into 2-cm/¾-inch pieces. Cut the chilli in half lengthways, remove the centre and finely chop. Peel the mangos, cut the flesh from the stone and cut into 3-cm/1¼-inch pieces. Peel the bananas and cut into 2-cm/¾-inch thick slices.

Heat the oil in a large frying pan. Fry the onion, coriander seeds, curry leaves, pepper and chilli on a low heat for 5 minutes, stirring occasionally. Add the cassava, banana and mango and cook for another 5-7 minutes.

Finally, add the double cream, 150 ml/⅔ cup water, lemon juice and soy sauce and leave to simmer on a low heat for a further 10 minutes, stirring occasionally. Season with salt and pepper.

TIPS
Serve with basmati rice. Instead of cassava, potatoes can also be used.

Cantonese Fried Rice

The popular Chinese street food

Preparation time:
30 minutes

Serves 4

250 g/1¼ cup basmati
rice
1 level tbsp salt
1 small head of broccoli
2 carrots
150 g/1 cup peas
100 g/⅓ cup canned
bamboo sprouts
200 g/2½ cups oyster
mushrooms
10 g/2 tsp fresh ginger
1 clove of garlic
5 tbsp neutral-flavoured
vegetable oil
5 tbsp soy sauce
Ground pepper

Cook the basmati rice in 1 litre/4¼ cups boiling water for 10-15 minutes, then drain, allow to dry and keep warm until needed.

Prepare the broccoli, wash and cut into small florets. Peel the carrots, cut into ½-cm/⅛-inch thick slices and cook in hot water for 3 minutes together with the broccoli. Then drain and put in a bowl. Add the peas and the bamboo shoots.

Prepare and wash the oyster mushrooms, cut into ½-cm/⅛-inch thick strips and put to one side. Peel the ginger and the garlic and cut into very thin pieces.

Heat the oil in a frying pan, add the oyster mushrooms, the garlic and the ginger and fry until golden brown. Add the vegetables and the rice and fry slowly for 5-8 minutes on a low heat. Finally, season with the soy sauce, salt and pepper.

TIPS
The vegetables can be varied depending on the season. The dish can be made spicier with sambal oelek, if liked.

Parsnip Gnocchi

Potato meets parsnip

Preparation time
1 hour

Serves 4

2 floury potatoes
4 parsnips
Salt
2 tbsp olive oil
Ground pepper, ground
nutmeg, chilli powder
200 g/1½ cups very strong
or first clear brown flour
200 g/3¼ cups
breadcrumbs
½ bunch chives
2 spring onions/scallions
Flour for the work
surface

TIPS
This could also be garnished
with a handful of pine nuts or
pumpkin seeds, almonds or poppy
seeds. Sprinkle with dried yeast
flakes for a cheese taste.

Peel the potatoes and the parsnips and cut into
1-cm/½-inch cubes. Cook the potatoes and half of the
parsnips in boiling, salted water for about 20 minutes
until soft. Drain and leave to steam.

Heat the oil in a frying pan and fry the remaining
parsnips on a medium heat until golden brown.
Remove the pan from the hob.

Mash the cooked potatoes and parsnips into a purée
with the potato masher. Season well with salt, pepper,
nutmeg and chilli powder. Mix in the brown flour and
the breadcrumbs and work everything into a dough.
Press the dough down flat and leave to cool in the fridge.

Cut the chives finely. Wash and prepare the spring
onions/scallions and finely chop.

Form the gnocchi dough into long rolls on a floured
surface. Cut into 2-cm/¾-inch pieces with a sharp
knife. Form these into oval-shaped balls with floured
hands and imprint with a fork.

Cook the gnocchi in portions in boiling, salted water
for about 4 minutes (they are done when they float to
the surface).

Heat up the parsnip pieces again on a medium heat.
Lift out the cooked gnocchi with a slotted spoon and
mix with the parsnip pieces in the pan. Season again
with salt and pepper and serve scattered with the
chives and the spring onions/scallions.

Tomato Spelt Risotto

Spelt rice is nutritious and has a wonderful nutty taste

Preparation time
1 hour

Serves 4

1 kg/2.2 lb tomatoes
2 shallots
1 tbsp neutral-flavoured
vegetable oil
1-2 tbsp tomato purée/
paste
200 g/1 cup spelt risotto
rice
1 level tsp salt
2 carrots
1 parsnip
200 g/1¼ cup cherry
tomatoes
1 bunch parsley
2 sprigs basil
80 ml/5 tbsp vegan
double cream
1 tsp nutritional yeast
flakes

Wash the tomatoes, remove the stalks and cut a cross on the bottom. Cover with boiling water, remove the skins, cut into quarters and remove the cores. Finely dice the fruit flesh.

Peel the shallots, cut into fine slices and fry in a large pan in the oil until they are soft. Add the tomato purée/paste and sauté lightly. Cover with 350 ml/1½ cups water and bring to the boil. Add the spelt risotto rice, bring to the boil again and season with a little salt. Leave to cook on a low heat for about 10 minutes, with the lid on.

In the meantime, peel the carrots and the parsnips and dice finely. Wash the cherry tomatoes, remove the stalks and cut in half. Finely chop the parsley and cut the plucked basil leaves into fine strips.

Add the carrots, parsnips and tomatoes to the spelt risotto and bring to the boil, stirring constantly, then reduce the heat. Simmer gently until the spelt rice is al dente. Add the double cream and season. Add the parsley, basil and the halved cherry tomatoes, serve the risotto in a dish, sprinkled with yeast flakes.

TIPS
Do not sauté the tomato purée/paste for too long, as it will become dark and taste bitter. Spelt risotto rice is a husked, light, ground spelt. It contains six times as much dietary fibre and double the amount of protein as white rice. You can buy it at well-stocked wholefood shops. Nutritional yeast flakes can also be bought in wholefood shops.

Baked Squash

Our favourite way to serve squash

Preparation time
35 minutes (including baking time)

Serves 4

1 small orange gourd or butternut squash
(1 kg/2.2 lb prepared weight)
2 sprigs rosemary
6 cloves of garlic
2 tbsp agave syrup
5 tbsp olive oil
Salt, ground pepper

Preheat the oven to 180°C/355°C.

Wash the squash, cut into quarters, remove the core and cut into about 2-cm/¾-inch pieces with the skin on. Pluck the rosemary. Peel the garlic and cut into fine pieces.

Mix the squash pieces with the rosemary needles, garlic, agave syrup and olive oil in a bowl. Season everything well with salt and pepper and arrange on a baking tray lined with baking paper. Bake the squash in the centre of the preheated oven for about 15 minutes.

TIP
Baked squash goes well with aubergine/eggplant and amaranth (page 18) and Peruvian quinoa salad (page 63).

Indonesian Tempeh with Vegetables

Fermented soy: the perfect health food

Preparation time
30 minutes
+ at least 3 hours'
marinating time

Serves 4

300 g/10 oz tempeh
1 stalk lemongrass
30 g/2 tbsp fresh ginger
3 tbsp teriyaki sauce
1 medium-sized head of
broccoli
Salt
2 spring onions/scallions
1 red bell pepper
2 pak choi
200 g/¾ cup bean
sprouts
80 ml/⅓ cup neutral-
flavoured vegetable oil

For the sauce
3 tbsp teriyaki sauce
3 tbsp soy sauce
100 g/½ cup peanut
butter
1-2 tbsp sambal oelek

Cut the tempeh in half lengthways, cut into 3-mm/⅛-inch thin slices and put in an oven-proof dish.

Bash the lemon grass flat at the lower end, peel the ginger, cut both into very thin slices and arrange on top of the tempeh strips. Pour the teriyaki sauce evenly over the top and marinate in the fridge for at least 3 hours.

Prepare and wash the broccoli, cut into florets and cook in salted water for 3-5 minutes, drain and put to one side. Wash and prepare the spring onions/scallions and cut lengthways into 3-cm/1¼-inch long pieces. Halve the peppers, remove the cores, wash and cut into ½-cm/⅛-inch wide strips. Wash the pak choi, cut in half and cut into 3-cm/1¼-inch pieces. Put the pak choi in a bowl together with the bean sprouts and the broccoli florets.

Fry the tempeh quickly with ginger and lemongrass as well as about 2 tbsp oil in a frying pan, until a crust forms, then put to one side. Put the remaining oil in the same pan and fry the vegetables quickly while tossing; they still need to be crunchy.

Add the ingredients for the sauce and 100 ml/7 tbsp water to the vegetables, bring to the boil and leave to simmer for 2-3 minutes. Add the tempeh to the vegetables, mix together and serve.

TIPS
Tempeh can be found in
wholefood shops. The tempeh can
also be marinated overnight for
great results.

The fundamentals: grains, pseudo-grains and legumes

The selection of protein-rich grain types is vast. As well as all of the wheat products, there are also **spelt, oats and barley** in an extraordinary number of varieties.

A nice contrast to the local grain types are the pseudo-grain types from South America, **amaranth** and **quinoa**. These nutritious varieties, which are particularly rich in protein, calcium and iron, have a long tradition in South American cooking and can be used in countless dishes such as salads, bakes and stews or also, in popped form, for muesli.

Just as useful is the wide variety of rice types which range from natural rice to whole-grain rice and the countless legumes which are irreplaceable in vegan cooking. The cooking of **peas, lentils** and **beans** can be very different. Those in a rush fall back on the shelled types such as red lentils, puy lentils or beluga lentils, the cooking time for which is no longer than quarter of an hour. Other dried legumes, on the other hand, have to be soaked for at least 8 hours and then cooked in unsalted water for 30 to 60 minutes. It is important to note that lentils or beans will not soften in salted water.

Those who cling to the old preconception that enjoying lentils and beans automatically leads to flatulence do not have to worry. This undesirable side-effect befalls only those who eat very little dietary fibre. Those who wish to take precautions should prepare their legumes with herbs such as fennel, caraway seeds, anise or savory, which are particularly mild and aid digestion.

Legumes can be used in an almost unlimited number of ways. They form a splendid foundation for any dish, whether for soups, stews, curries, dips or rissoles. A special bonus: the large variety of shapes and colours of legumes are not only enjoyable to eat, but also to look at.

Dal Pancharangi

Eat with a Bollywood film

Preparation time:
1 hour

Serves 4

5 g/1 tsp fresh ginger
1 small pepperoncini
(mild chilli)
1 onion
1 clove of garlic
2 tbsp neutral-flavoured
vegetable oil
1 pinch ground
cinnamon
2 pinches ground
coriander
2 pinches ground cumin
1 pinch mild paprika
1 pinch garam masala
1 level tsp caster/
superfine sugar
1 tbsp tomato purée/
paste
600 ml/2½ cups water
200 ml/¾ cup vegetable
stock
300 g/10 oz dal mixture,
consisting of 60 g/2 oz
each of tool dal, chana
dal, urad dal, brown
lentils and whole mung
beans
1 bayleaf
½ tsp salt
1 pinch chilli powder
2 tomatoes

Peel the ginger and dice finely. Cut the chillies in half, remove the cores, wash and cut into fine strips. Peel the onion and the garlic and chop finely.

Heat the oil and fry the prepared ingredients for 1-2 minutes. Add the spices, sugar and tomato purée/paste and fry for a further 30 seconds.

Add the water and the vegetable stock and bring to the boil. Add the lentil mixture and the bayleaf and season with salt and chilli powder. Leave to simmer for 30-40 minutes. If necessary add water. The dal should still be slightly crunchy.

Wash the tomatoes, remove the stalks, dice finely, add to the dal and cook for a further 5 minutes. Season with salt and pepper.

TIP
At the end, squeeze some lime juice over the dish. The lentils can be found in well-stocked wholefood and Indian food shops. For those suffering from allergies: asafoetida (devil's dirt) can be used instead of onion and garlic.

Singapore Noodles

They taste best straight from the wok

Preparation time
30 minutes

Serves 4

200 g/2¼ cups rice
noodles (vermicelli)
1-2 tbsp sambal oelek
8 tbsp neutral-flavoured
vegetable oil
300 g/10 oz tofu
10 g/3 tsp fresh ginger
200 g/3¼ cups shiitake
mushrooms
2 spring onions
200 g/1 cup fresh or
frozen soya beans
100 g/ 6 tbsp
beansprouts
Salt
1 tbsp tamarind paste
60 ml/5 tbsp soy sauce
Salt, ground pepper
½ bunch fresh coriander/
cilantro

Leave the rice noodles to soften in lukewarm water for 5 minutes. Then cool them under cold running water and allow to drain well. Immediately mix in the sambal oelek and 2 tbsp oil so that the noodles do not stick during frying.

Cut the tofu into 1-cm/⅜-inch cubes. Peel the ginger and cut into fine strips. Wash the shiitake mushrooms, cut away the stalks and cut the mushrooms into 3-mm/⅛-inch fine strips. Wash and prepare the spring onions/scallions and cut into 3-mm/⅛-inch fine strips.

Blanch the soy beans in boiling salted water or steam for 2 minutes.

Heat 6 tbsp oil in a large frying pan or in a wok. Fry the diced tofu and the ginger for 2 minutes. Add the shiitake mushrooms, spring onions/scallions and beansprouts and fry for a further 2-4 minutes. Then add the noodles and the soy beans and fry for 3-5 minutes, stirring constantly.

Dissolve the tamarind paste in 150 ml/⅔ cup water and add to the noodles together with the soy sauce. Bring to the boil, season with salt and pepper and garnish with the plucked coriander/cilantro leaves. Serve immediately.

TIP
Tamarind paste can be found in wholefood shops or in Asian food shops.

Aloo Bhaji

An Indian classic

Preparation time
30 minutes

Serves 4

1 kg/2.2 lbs waxy
potatoes
3 small green chillies
2 tbsp neutral-flavoured
vegetable oil
1 tsp ground turmeric
1 tsp ground asafoetida
½ tsp brown mustard seeds
1 tsp poppy seeds
1 tsp cumin seeds
15 curry leaves
600 ml/2½ cups
vegetable stock
1 tsp ground coriander
1 tsp ground cumin
Salt, ground pepper, raw
cane sugar
4 sprigs of fresh
coriander/cilantro

Peel the potatoes and cut into 2-cm/¾-inch pieces. Cut away the stalks of the chillies and chop finely.

Heat the oil in a pan. Add the spices up to and including the curry leaves and carefully fry on a medium heat, stirring occasionally, until the mustard and poppy seeds begin to bounce and release a delicate aroma. Add the potatoes and fry. Cover with the stock and cook the potatoes for 10-15 minutes until soft, stirring occasionally.

Stir in the ground coriander and cumin. Season with salt, pepper and sugar. Chop the fresh coriander/cilantro finely and sprinkle over the aloo bhaji.

TIPS
2 tbsp roasted sesame seeds or a handful of roasted cashew nuts work well as a garnish. This curry goes well with the beetroot and apple salad (page 73) or the tomato and tofu sambal (page 102). A finely chopped clove of garlic can be used as an alternative to the Indian seasoning, asafoetida. Asafoetida and curry leaves can be bought in Asian food shops.

Green Thai Aubergine/Eggplant Curry

With coconut milk and kaffir limes for lovers of Thai cooking

Preparation time
30 minutes (including baking time)

Serves 4

3 large aubergines/
eggplants or 5-6 Thai
aubergines/eggplants
1 level tbsp salt
6-7 tbsp neutral-
flavoured vegetable oil
2 red bell peppers
2 kaffir lime leaves
600ml/2½ cups coconut
milk
80 g/3 oz green Thai
curry paste
Salt, ground pepper

Preheat the fan oven to 180°C/355°F.

Wash and prepare the aubergines/eggplants and cut into 2-cm/¾-inch pieces. Mix the aubergine/eggplant pieces with the salt and 3-4 tbsp oil and arrange on a baking tray lined with baking paper. Bake in the preheated oven for 10-13 minutes and put to one side.

In the meantime, cut the bell peppers in half, remove the centres, wash and cut into ½-cm/⅛-inch wide strips. Heat 3 tbsp oil in a frying pan and fry the pepper strips with the kaffir lime leaves on a low heat for 3-5 minutes, occasionally turning. Add the aubergine/eggplant pieces and fry quickly.

Add the coconut milk and the green Thai curry paste and leave the curry to simmer on a low heat for 5-8 minutes. Season with salt and pepper.

TIP
Use more or less curry paste depending on how hot you like your curry. Freshly cut coriander/cilantro is a good garnish. Basmati rice or couscous are suitable accompaniments. You can also add tofu cubes or green beans to the curry.

Kabuli Palaw

A secret Persian recipe

Preparation time
40 minutes

Serves 4

1 tsp saffron threads
600 ml/2½ cups
lukewarm vegetable
stock
2 onions
4 tbsp olive oil
300 g/1½ cups basmati
rice
30 g/1 oz tomato purée/
paste
Salt
2 small carrots
100 g/½ cup almonds
100 g/½ cup pistachios
60 g/7 tbsp raisins
4 tbsp raw cane sugar
2 tsp garam masala
Ground pepper

Leave the saffron threads to soak in the lukewarm stock. Peel the onions and chop finely. Heat 2 tbsp oil in a pan and glaze the onions on a medium heat. Mix in the rice and fry for 2 minutes. Stir in the tomato purée/paste and fry for a further 2 minutes.

Add the soaked saffron threads together with the stock to the rice, add salt and bring to the boil. When the broth is boiling, remove the pan from the hob and leave the rice for about 20 minutes to completely infuse with the lid on.

In the meantime, peel the carrots and cut into fine strips with a potato peeler or a grater. Heat the remaining oil in a frying pan; caramelize the almonds, pistachios and raisins with the sugar on a medium heat while stirring. Mix in the carrot strips.

When the rice is cooked, mix in the carrot mixture and heat up again with the lid on. Season with garam masala, salt and pepper.

TIPS
Palaw (depending on the country, written as pilaf, pilav, polo, palov or pilau) refers to the cooking technique with which the rice is steamed with stock, seasoning and other ingredients such as, for example, vegetables, fruit and nuts. A palaw is considered particularly successful if a crunchy crust forms on the bottom.

Chilli and Bean Stew

Chilli sin carne

Preparation time
1 hour + soaking time
overnight

Serves 4

60 g/¼ cup white beans
60 g/¼ cup seasonal
beans
150 g/¾ cup kidney
beans
2 small green chillies
1 large onion
2 cloves of garlic
2 red bell peppers
3 tbsp olive oil
15 g/½ oz tomato purée/
paste
100 g/3½ oz soy mince
30 g/1 oz bulgar wheat
1 tbsp cider vinegar
1 litre/4¼ cups vegetable
stock
1 tbsp mild paprika
½ tsp ground chilli
1 carrot
1 waxy potato
80 g pickled gherkins
½ bunch fresh coriander/
cilantro
100 g/½ cup sweetcorn
50 g/¼ cup vegan double
cream
Salt, ground pepper

Soak the legumes separately overnight in three times as much water. The next day, cook separately in fresh, unsalted water for about 40-50 minutes (depending on the type), until soft. Drain and leave to dry.

In the meantime, cut away the stalks of the chillies and chop finely. Peel the onion and garlic and again chop finely. Cut the bell peppers in half, remove the centres, wash and dice finely.

Heat the oil in a pan. Fry the onion, garlic, chilli and pepper on a medium heat, stirring occasionally. Add the tomato purée/paste and the soy mince and fry for a few minutes. Add the bulgar, cider vinegar, vegetable stock and paprika and chilli powder and bring to the boil.

Peel the carrot and potato and grate into fine strips, stir into the chilli and cook for 10-15 minutes on a medium heat until soft. Cut the pickled gherkins into fine strips, chop the coriander/cilantro finely.

When the vegetables are soft, stir in the cooked beans with the sweetcorn and the vegan double cream. Season with salt and pepper and bring to the boil once more. Sprinkle with the pickled gherkins and the finely chopped coriander/cilantro and serve.

TIPS
The longer this chilli is boiled down, the better it tastes. It is therefore a good idea to prepare it a day in advance. It is best to prepare double the amount and freeze half. This goes well with rice or corn tortillas.

Aubergine/Eggplant Cordon Bleu

Guaranteed to impress dinner guests

Preparation time
40 minutes (including baking time)

Serves 4

2-3 medium-sized aubergines/eggplants
Salt, ground pepper
400 g/3¼ cups vegan cheese
2-3 tomatoes
2-3 sprigs of fresh thyme
2 tbsp cornflour/ cornstarch
150 g/2½ cups vegan breadcrumbs
6-8 tbsp neutral-flavoured vegetable oil for frying

Wash and prepare the aubergines/eggplants, cut in half and then lengthways into ½-cm/⅛-inch thin slices. Lay out pairs of slices which fit together in terms of size. Arrange on a work surface. Season well with salt and pepper.

Cut the cheese into very thin slices and arrange on one half of the aubergines/eggplants. Wash the tomatoes, remove the stalks, cut in half and then into 3-mm/⅜-inch slices and arrange on top of the cheese. Pluck the thyme leaves and sprinkle on top of the tomato slices. Cover with the remaining aubergine/eggplant slices.

Stir the cornflour/cornstarch with 4-5 tbsp water; put the breadcrumbs in a deep plate. Carefully roll the prepared aubergine/eggplant cordon bleus first in the cornflour/cornstarch, then in the breadcrumbs and press these on. Fix with a tooth pick, if needed. Heat plenty of oil in a frying pan and fry the aubergines/eggplants on both sides for a few minutes until golden brown. Lay on the baking tray lined with baking paper and bake in the pre-heated oven at 180°C/355°F for 7-12 minutes.

TIPS
Serve the cordon bleus on a tomato coulis or with vegan herb butter. Cordon bleus can be prepared and fried in advance; finish off in the oven before serving. The 'no-moo' cheese which can be bought in wholefood shops is excellent for cordon bleus.

Hiltl

DESSERTS

Classy, fruity, creamy and sweet:
Desserts which leave nothing
to be desired

The cow should not have the monopoly on milk

Milk alternatives are abundant. They are made from spelt, oats, rice, quinoa, amaranth, soy or almonds and are available in wholefood shops, and increasingly in supermarkets and corner stores. There is no formula as to what milk is right for you, but this can also be a good thing: it's a lot of fun to find out which of the very different aromas and consistencies of each product you like the best from the large range. For vegans, we recommend milk drinks that are enriched with calcium and vitamin B12. Spelt, oat, rice and almond drinks have a low protein content. If you prefer soya drinks, we recommend those which are made from organic soya so that you are sure that the product is GMO-free.

Admittedly, strawberries and cream are a wonderful combination. However, you do not necessarily need cream made from cow's milk for this. Those who love sauces and soups refined with cream can turn to **cream alternatives** such as soy, rice, oat or spelt cream without a problem, or, as in Southeast Asia, to coconut milk. This, however, has a strong taste which you have to think about when seasoning each different dish. Vegan double creams are available in wholefood shops, but often also in the supermarket. Back to the strawberries: vegan whipping cream and squirty cream in a can may be found in many health-food stores and in wholefood shops. When buying vegan whipping cream, you should check whether the product will need a cream setter.

Butter to spread on bread can be replaced with vegetable margarine without a problem – in most cases. It is worth checking the list of ingredients carefully. Sometimes traces of milk protein, yoghurt or fatty acids can be found in supposedly vegan margarine. Also, vitamin D, which is often made from lanolin, is sometimes an uninvited guest in products which otherwise originate purely from vegetables.

When you bake, do not just replace the butter with margarine, but use vegetable oil as well – nut oil, rapeseed oil and olive oil are not only fit for purpose, but also add to the wonderful smell of the baked goods.

Yoghurt lovers can find a wide range of similar soy-based products in specialist shops. Many of these are produced with bacterial cultures and come in many different flavours. Rice-based yoghurt alternatives can also be bought, but only in better-stocked shops.

Those who love set yoghurt as a dessert can strain natural soy yoghurt or vegan cream cheese using a sieve or towel in order to obtain a firmer texture. Thicker textures are often excellent for dips and spreads.

The powerful, unmistakable taste of **cheese** can also be produced nowadays without using milk from animals. There are many types of vegan cheese, from hard cheese to creamy mozzarella and everything in between, the taste of which is impressively close to the original. Vegan types of cheese, however, contain neither calcium nor protein, which must be considered along with its nutritional value.

If you are looking for a vegan replacement for grated cheese (for example for pasta or risotto), dried yeast flakes are suitable for this, which have a full, rounded taste – and which additionally contain useful B vitamins.

Cheesecakes that are made with tofu have some particularly tempting results – that is with a mixture of natural tofu, which has been puréed with silken tofu. This mixture is then seasoned with sugar, lemon juice and vanilla extract and baked on vegan shortcrust pastry. It is definitely worth a try: even hard-core cheesecake lovers won't notice that their favourite dish has been made in a different way.

Silken Tofu Mousse with Berries

An elegant combination and a sweet temptation

Preparation time
30 minutes

Serves 4

300 g/2 cups
strawberries
1 tbsp raw cane sugar
Ground black pepper
1 vanilla pod
250g/9 oz silken tofu
100 g/¾ cup icing/
confectioner's sugar
200g/7 oz vegan
whipping cream
200g/7 oz vegan biscuits
2 tbsp amaretto

Wash the strawberries, remove the stalks and cut into quarters or eighths depending on the size, and mix carefully in a bowl with the sugar and three twists of freshly ground pepper.

Cut the vanilla pod in half lengthways and scrape out the seeds. Purée the vanilla in a tall container with the hand blender, together with the silken tofu and the icing/confectioner's sugar. Beat the whipping cream until stiff and mix into the silken tofu cream.

Wrap the vegan biscuits in a clean kitchen cloth and roll over with a rolling pin to make large crumbs. Add the crumbs to a bowl and moisten with amaretto.

Layer the ingredients in glasses or bowls, first the strawberries, then the silken tofu cream and finally the broken biscuits.

TIPS
This dessert can be prepared a day in advance. Then break up the biscuits shortly before serving and sprinkle over the top, as otherwise they will be soft. Alternatively, the vegan sponge mixture (page 215) can be broken up or cut out in circles, moistened with amaretto and layered with the silken tofu and the berries in the glasses. Orange or coffee liqueurs can also be used instead of amaretto. Silken tofu is available in health-food shops, supermarkets and in Asian food shops.

Spiced Chocolate Cake

Tastes like Christmas!

Preparation time
About 1 hour (including baking time)

For 1 large loaf tin
(about 35 cm/14 inches in length)

250 g/2 cups white flour
40 g/7 tbsp cocoa powder
½ tsp salt
2 tsp baking powder
200 g/1 cup raw cane sugar
3 tbsp garam masala
100 ml/½ cup neutral-flavoured vegetable oil
2 tbsp white balsamic vinegar
Vegetable margarine and flour for the tin
Icing/confectioner's sugar for dusting

Preheat the oven to 180°C/355°F. Grease the cake tin with vegetable margarine and coat with flour or line with baking paper.

Mix the flour in a bowl for a few minutes with the cocoa powder, salt, baking powder, sugar and garam masala. Mix the oil, balsamic vinegar and 200 ml/13½ tbsp of sparkling water with the baking powder in a bowl, then add to the flour mixture and stir with an electric hand whisk.

Fill the loaf tin with the batter and bake in the middle of the preheated oven for 40-50 minutes. Test with a skewer; if it does not come out clean, cook for a few more minutes.

Leave the cake to cool in the tin for a few minutes, then tip out, remove the baking paper and dust the cake with icing/confectioner's sugar. It tastes great warm or cold.

TIPS
Instead of garam masala, you could also use five spice powder, gingerbread or honey cake spices. The cake tastes even better when it is prepared a day in advance and covered with tin foil overnight to infuse.

Saffron Semolina Pudding

Indian sweet

Preparation time
30 minutes

Serves 4

500 ml/2 cups almond
milk
2 pinches saffron threads
150 ml/10 tbsp mild olive
oil
150 g/¾ cup durum
wheat semolina
100 g/½ cup raw cane
sugar
2 pinches ground
cardamom
45 g/¼ cup raisins
30 g/3 tbsp pistachios

Heat the almond milk and allow the saffron threads to infuse in it for 5 minutes.

Heat the oil in a pan and roast the durum wheat semolina on a medium heat, stirring constantly, until it becomes fragrant. Reduce the heat, add the sugar and allow to melt, stirring occasionally. Add the almond milk with the saffron threads to the semolina and stir in well so that no lumps form. Mix in the cardamom and raisins and bring the semolina pudding to the boil.

Simmer on a medium heat for about 15 minutes until the semolina is soft, stirring occasionally.

Chop the pistachios finely and dry roast in a pan. Serve the saffron semolina pudding with the pistachios sprinkled over the top.

TIPS
The raisins and pistachios can be replaced with other dried fruits, for example goji berries or barberries, and other nuts such as almonds, chufas or walnuts. As an alternative to almond milk, soya, rice, oat or spelt milk is also suitable. Saffron is the most expensive spice in the world because the stigmas (three pieces per flower) must be picked by hand. Be sure to use saffron sparingly, as otherwise it has a bitter taste.

Sticky Toffee Pudding

The most popular dessert in our London restaurant. Careful, it's sweet!

Preparation time
1 hour 10 minutes
(including baking time)

Serves 4

6-7 fresh dates
3 g/½ tsp fresh ginger
130 g/½ cup vegetable
margarine
50 g/¼ cup raw cane
sugar
130 ml/½ cup soya milk
1 espresso cup of Italian
espresso
100 g/¾ cup white flour
½ tsp baking powder
1 pinch ground nutmeg
1 pinch ground
cinnamon

For the sauce
80 ml/6 tbsp maple
syrup
50 g/¼ cup raw cane
sugar
80 ml/⅓ cup vegan
whipping cream

Preheat the oven to 140°C/285°F.

Cut the dates in half, remove the pits and cut into ½-cm/¼-inch thick slices. Peel the ginger and finely slice. Mix the dates and ginger with the margarine and the raw cane sugar to form a smooth mixture. Add the remaining ingredients and fold into the date mixture.

Fill a non-greased cake tin with the mixture and bake in the middle of the preheated oven for 40-50 minutes.

In the meantime, boil down the ingredients for the sauce by half in a small pan on a low heat for 5-8 minutes. Pour the warm sauce over the still warm pudding and allow to cool.

TIP
The toffee can be eaten warm or cold and with any fresh fruit or a scoop of ice cream. The toffee pudding tastes even better the next day.

Mango Cake

Fruity and tempting

Preparation time
1 hour and 30 minutes
(including baking time)

For 2 loaf tins, about 17
cm/7 inches in length

2 ripe mangos
100 g/¾ cup white flour
30 g/5 tbsp spelt flour
30 g/5 tbsp cornflour/
cornstarch
190 g/1 cup raw cane
sugar
7 g/2 tsp baking powder
5 g/1 tsp bicarbonate of
soda
75 g/1 cup desiccated
coconut
130 ml/½ cup rice milk
90 ml/6 tbsp neutral-
flavoured vegetable oil

Preheat the oven to 180°C/355°F.

Peel the mangos, cut the flesh from the stone and cut into about 1-cm/½-inch cubes. Put the remaining ingredients in a bowl and mix thoroughly. Add the mango pieces and mix through evenly.

Put the mixture into the loaf tins lined with baking paper straight away and bake in the preheated oven for about 1 hour. Important: do not open the oven at all during the baking time!

Take the cakes out of the oven and leave to cool for 30 minutes, then lift out of the tins with the baking paper and allow to cool on a wire rack.

TIP
Be sure not to use too large a cake tin, so it rises well and keeps its shape.

Sweet Polenta Bake with Rhubarb Compote

A dessert you can adapt for all seasons

Preparation time
50 minutes (including
baking time)

Serves 4

500 ml/2 cups soy milk
4 tbsp raw cane sugar
50 g sultanas
100 g/3½ oz polenta
1 pinch ground vanilla
200 ml/13½ tbsp vegan
whipping cream
2 apples

For the compote
6 stalks of rhubarb
120 g/10 tbsp sugar
3 tbsp blackcurrant
syrup

Preheat the oven to 180°C/355°F.

Put the soy milk, sugar, sultanas, polenta and vanilla in a pan and cook on a low heat for 3-5 minutes, stirring occasionally, until it thickens. Take the pan off the hob and allow the mixture to cool, stirring occasionally.

Beat the whipping cream until stiff. Wash the apples, remove the cores and grate with a grater. Add to the polenta mixture together with the whipped cream. Mix everything well and tip into a cake tin.

Bake in the preheated oven for 20-25 minutes. The gratin is still soft after baking but will stiffen up while cooling.

For the compote, wash the rhubarb, remove the threads, cut into 2-cm/¾-inch long pieces and put in a pan. Add the sugar, 100 ml/7 tbsp water and the blackcurrant syrup and cook on a low heat with the lid on, stirring occasionally, until the consistency is that of a compote.

Serve the compote with the gratin. The gratin can be eaten both warm and cold.

TIPS
Other fruit can be used for the
compote depending on the season.
The sultanas can also be left out
depending on taste.

Pomegranate Granita

The perfect cooler on a hot day

Preparation time
20 minutes
+ freezing time

Serves 4

400 ml/1⅔ cups
pomegranate juice
70 g/6 tbsp raw cane
sugar
1 pomegranate
Juice of ½ lime

Heat the pomegranate juice with the sugar until the sugar has melted.

Cut the pomegranate in half and remove the seeds into a bowl. The best way to do this is by using water: press the pomegranate into the water with the cut surface facing downwards and release the seeds by breaking apart the skin with your fingers. The seeds sink to the bottom of the bowl and the white skin floats to the top and can be scooped out.

Mix the lime juice and the pomegranate seeds into the pomegranate juice. Put everything into an ice-cream maker and allow to freeze. Serve immediately.

TIP
If you don't have an ice-cream maker, you can also freeze the granita in the freezer. To do this, fill a freezer-proof plastic bowl with the cooled liquid and freeze for at least 3-4 hours. Stir every 30 minutes until it is solid so that the mixture freezes evenly.

Cinnamon and Mandarin Panna Cotta

Lighter than the traditional dessert

Preparation time
35 minutes
+ cooling time

Serves 4

For the panna cotta
400 ml/1⅔ cups soy
double cream
150 ml/⅔ cup almond
milk
1 pinch ground vanilla
2-3 pinches agar agar
powder
3 tbsp raw cane sugar
1 pinch ground
cinnamon

For the sauce
700 g/25 oz mandarins
1 tsp cornflour/
cornstarch
3 tbsp raw cane sugar
1 tbsp lemon juice

Put the ingredients for the panna cotta in a pan and bring to the boil, stirring regularly. Remove the pan from the hob and allow the mixture to cool. In the meantime stir with a whisk so that no skin forms.

Put the lukewarm mixture into moulds, cover with cling film and leave to cool in the fridge for at least 6 hours.

For the sauce, cut the mandarins in half, squeeze the juice and put in a pan. Add the remaining ingredients, mix well with the whisk, bring to the boil while stirring and allow to cool.

TIPS
The panna cotta can be prepared a day in advance. Use mandarin segments to garnish which have been caramelized in margarine and sugar. Depending on the season, other fruits can be used, for example, fresh raspberries, strawberries, etc.

Indian Chai Tea Cream

Melts in the mouth

Preparation time
30 minutes
+ cooling time

Serves 4

100 g/½ cup caster/
superfine sugar
12 g/8 tsp chai tea
mixture (about the
amount from 4 tea bags)
3 g/2 tsp black tea (about
the amount from 1 tea
bag)
200 ml/¾ cup almond
milk
3-4 level tbsp cornflour/
cornstarch
400 ml/1⅔ cups vegan
whipping cream
Chocolate powder and
almond brittle to garnish

Bring 400 ml/1⅔ cups water and the sugar to the boil in a pan. Add the tea in a tea infuser and leave to infuse for about 15 minutes. Remove the tea infuser from the liquid, drain well and bring the liquid to the boil again.

In the meantime, mix the almond milk thoroughly with the cornflour/cornstarch in a bowl and add to the boiling tea. Bring the cream to the boil again, constantly stirring, and remove from the hob (be careful, danger of spitting!). Fill a bowl with the cream and allow to cool, stirring occasionally.

Beat the whipping cream until stiff and carefully fold into the cooled tea cream. Put the tea cream in glasses or on plates and garnish with chocolate powder and almond brittle.

TIPS
Chai tea mixtures can be found in any good tea shop. The tea cream can be cooked the evening before. It is important to then mix it well the next day and fold the stiff whipping cream into it carefully.

Coconut rice pudding

An exotic dream dessert

Preparation time
1 hour

Serves 4

200 g/1 cup round-grain rice
800 ml/3⅓ cups coconut milk
100 g/½ cup palm sugar
50 g/10 tbsp desiccated coconut
30 g/¼ cup cashews
1 tsp ground cardamom
30 g/3 tbsp raisins

Rinse the rice and allow to drain. Put in a pan with the coconut milk and bring to the boil slowly with the lid on.

Crush the palm sugar roughly using a pestle and mortar, add to the simmering rice and melt while stirring. Stir in the desiccated coconut and allow the rice to simmer for 35-40 minutes on a low heat and with the lid on until the rice is soft. Stir occasionally so that nothing sticks – you may need to stir in another 100 ml/7 tbsp water.

In the meantime, dry roast the cashews in a pan, then chop roughly. When the rice is cooked, stir in the cardamom and the raisins. Sprinkle the coconut rice pudding with the chopped cashews.

TIP
Pistachios, sunflower seeds or pine nuts also taste good instead of cashews.

Exotic spring rolls

A true test of your rolling skills

Preparation time

1 hour (including baking time)

Makes 16 spring rolls

¼ pineapple
Juice of ½ lime
50 g/¼ cup palm sugar
50 g/1¾ oz marzipan paste
70 g/1 cup desiccated coconut
16 spring roll wrappers, 10 x 10 cm/4 x 4 inches
2 tbsp vegetable margarine

TIPS
If you want to make this even more exotic, the spring rolls can be brushed with a little coconut oil instead of vegetable margarine. These go well with the pomegranate granita (page 159), fresh fruit salad or a blob of vegan whipping cream.

Peel the pineapple and dice finely. Bring the lime juice to the boil in a pan with 100 ml/7 tbsp water. Add the palm sugar and melt it in the mixture. Mix in the pineapple pieces and simmer on a low heat for about 2 minutes.

Add the marzipan paste and simmer, stirring occasionally until it has dissolved. Stir in the desiccated coconut and keep stirring until the entire liquid is absorbed. Allow the mixture to cool.

Preheat the oven to 180°C/355°F.

Lay a spring roll wrapper on a cutting board and sprinkle lightly with water. Put 1 tbsp filling in the middle of the lower half of the sheet – leave 1½-cm/½-inch gap from the lower, left-hand and right-hand edge. Sprinkle the edges with a little water. First fold the two free left- and right-hand edges inwards over the filling, then fold the lower edge over the filling and roll the spring roll up to the upper free edge. Repeat until all of the wrappers have been used.

Melt the vegetable margarine gently in a pan. Put the spring rolls on a baking tray lined with baking paper and brush with the liquid vegetable margarine. Bake in the middle of the preheated oven for 15-20 minutes until golden brown. Serve warm.

Pineapple Crumble

Sweet and crisp out of the oven

Preparation time
50 minutes (including
baking time)

Makes 1 cake tin, serves 4

½ pineapple
1 tbsp raw cane sugar
200 g/1½ cups
wholemeal flour
200 g/1 cup raw cane
sugar
1 tsp ground turmeric
200 g/¾ cup soft
vegetable margarine
100 g/1¼ cup desiccated
coconut
Vegetable margarine for
the tin

Grease a cake tin with vegetable margarine. Peel the pineapple thoroughly and cut into 2-cm/½-inch pieces. Mix with the tablespoon of raw cane sugar in a bowl.

Mix the flour with the sugar, turmeric, margarine and desiccated coconut. Mix into breadcrumbs with the dough hooks on the electric hand whisk and then with your hands.

Preheat the oven to 200°C/390°F.

Arrange the pineapple in the greased cake tin and sprinkle with the crumbs of dough. Bake the pineapple crumble in the middle of the preheated oven for around 25 minutes until golden brown. Serve warm.

TIPS
For variety, flavour the pineapple with alcohol. Coconut and orange liqueurs work well. This goes well with a light, soft vegan ice cream or sorbet.

Soya Chocolate Mousse

Chocolatey, creamy, rich

Preparation time
45 minutes
+ cooling time

Serves 4

140 g/¾ cup vegan dark
couverture chocolate (70%)
140 g/¾ cup vegan dark
couverture chocolate (49%)
150 ml/⅔ cup soy milk
500 g/18 oz silken tofu
160 g/¾ cup raw cane
sugar
2 tsp locust bean gum
250 ml/1 cup vegan
whipping cream
50 g/½ cup vegan grated
couverture chocolate (49%)

Slowly melt the couvertures with the soya milk in a bowl over a hot water bath.

At the same time, purée the silken tofu, sugar and locust bean gum in a tall container with the hand blender. Slowly add the silken tofu mixture to the melted couvertures, stirring constantly. Leave the chocolate mixture to cool to room temperature.

Beat the vegan whipping cream with the electric whisk in a bowl until stiff and carefully fold into the cooled chocolate mixture with the couverture gratings to create a marbling effect. Leave the chocolate mousse to cool for at least 2 hours.

TIPS
The chocolate mousse will be solid after 1 hour in the freezer. Instead of the different couvertures, if liked, other sorts can also be used. Vegan couvertures can be obtained in health-food shops and in specialist shops. In the case of couvertures from the supermarket, always study the ingredients list well to ensure that it is in fact vegan.

tibits

BREAKFAST AND DRINKS

Classic, crunchy and refined:
Breakfast and drinks to set
you up for a good day

Leave the eggs to the hens. We are already one step ahead.

We begin with breakfast. Those who are used to starting the day with creamy **scrambled eggs** can still do this the vegan way. The magic word is tofu, more specifically an elegant mixture of natural and silken tofu. The natural tofu is seasoned and coloured with turmeric, broken up with a fork and fried for a few minutes in a little oil. The puréed silken tofu is mixed into the natural tofu. Then the tofu scrambled eggs are seasoned with salt and pepper and sprinkled with chives, spring onions/scallions and, if liked, chopped tomatoes. A good tip for everyone who particularly likes good aromas: if you replace half of the salt with kala namak, black Indian salt, your vegan breakfast takes on the most amazing taste.

Also, breaded dishes can be adapted to the vegan way of life without a problem. Replace the beaten egg with 1 tablespoon of cornflour/cornstarch or even with spelt, soy or chickpea flour, mixed with 3 tablespoons of soya milk or water. This mixture makes superfluous not only eggs, but also the countless powdered egg substitutes that can be found in health-food shops – these fulfil their purpose, but are, as rule, processed products which contain additives which are best gone without.

A hot topic for many is that of vegan **baking**. In vegan cooking, the egg is replaced by soya flour or additional baking powder: 1 tablespoon soya flour or 1 teaspoon baking powder take on the function of an egg. In fruit cakes or bread dough, linseeds or chia seeds puréed with a little water can take on the binding function of the egg – or, even more simply, apple purée or a mashed banana.

Light sponge mixture can also be made in the vegan way without a fuss. Sparkling mineral water supplies the carbon dioxide which makes the mixture light and fluffy (see the recipe on page 215). The same trick can also be used to make vegan pancakes. For cake glazes and fillings, you can again try the trusted mixture of silken and natural tofu, see above.

Cranberry Granola

For a joyful start to the day

Preparation time
25 minutes (including baking time)

Serves 4

100 g/1¼ cups coarse oats
80 g/½ cup unblanched almonds
25 g/1 oz pumpkin seeds
25 g/1 oz sunflower seeds
25 g/3 tbsp wheatgerm
1 pinch ground cloves
1 pinch ground cinnamon
1 pinch ground cardamon
1½ tbsp neutral-flavoured vegetable oil
3 tbsp maple syrup
1 tbsp agave syrup
120 g/1¼ cups dried cranberries

Preheat the oven to 170°C/340°F.

Mix the oats, almonds, pumpkin and sunflower seeds and wheatgerm. Mix in the ground cloves, cinnamon and cardamom.

Mix in the oil, the maple syrup and the agave syrup and spread the mixture on a baking tray lined with baking paper.

Bake the granola in the centre of the preheated oven for about 15 minutes. Leave to cool for a few minutes, then break up gently and mix in the cranberries.

TIPS
The cranberry granola tastes great with fresh fruit, soy yoghurt or milk alternatives with a grainy aroma, for example almond or oat milk. Packed up nicely, the cranberry granola makes a lovely gift.

Strawberry and Banana Salad

Refreshingly summery

Preparation time
20 minutes

Serves 4

400 g/2½ cups
strawberries
2 medium-sized bananas
1 tbsp lemon juice
100 g/7 tbsp natural soy
yoghurt
2 tbsp agave syrup
Five-spice powder

Wash the strawberries, remove the stalks and cut into quarters or eighths depending on the size. Peel the bananas, cut into slices and immediately sprinkle with lemon juice so that they don't go brown.

Mix the soy yoghurt with the agave syrup and 1 pinch of five-spice powder. Carefully fold in the bananas and the strawberries. Dust the strawberry and banana salad with a little five-spice powder and serve.

TIP
Five-spice powder is a Chinese spice mixture containing, among other things, star anise, Sichuan pepper, cinnamon, cloves and fennel seeds. It brings a warm, Christmassy aroma to desserts, cakes and biscuits. Five-spice powder can be bought in wholefood shops, Asian shops and well-stocked supermarkets. Alternatively, gingerbread spices can be used.

Mint and Kiwi Lemonade

The ideal refreshment for a hot day

Preparation time
20 minutes

For 500 ml/2 cups syrup,
enough for 12 portions of
lemonade

For the syrup
2-3 kiwis
4-5 sprigs mint
Juice of 2 lemons
100 ml/7 tbsp elderflower
syrup
4 tbsp caster/superfine
sugar

**For 1 portion of
lemonade (300ml/1¼
cups)**
40 ml/4 dessert spoons
syrup
1-2 ice cubes
150 ml/⅔ cup still or
sparkling mineral water
Fresh mint and kiwi
slices for garnish

Peel the kiwis and cut into quarters. Wash the mint, shake dry and pluck the leaves.

Put all of the ingredients for the syrup together with 100 ml/7 tbsp water in a food processor and mix on the highest setting for about 30 seconds. Fill a bottle with the finished syrup and store somewhere cool.

For 1 portion of mint and kiwi lemonade you will need 40ml/4 dessert spoons of syrup. Put the syrup in a glass, add the ice cubes and fill up with still or sparkling mineral water, depending on taste. Mix well. Garnish with mint and a slice of kiwi.

TIP
The syrup can be stored in the fridge for 2-3 days.

Green Power

Green energy in a glass

Preparation time
20 minutes

Makes 2 litres/8½ cups

2 kg/4½ lb apples
1 kg/2.2 lb fennel
50 g/1¾ oz wheatgrass
Juice of 1 lemon

Wash the apples, cut into quarters and remove the cores. Wash the fennel heads, cut in half, cut away the hard stalk and the long tips. Put the apple and the fennel into the juicer in portions.

Wash the wheatgrass and shake dry. Mix all of the ingredients together and purée with the hand blender or food processor.

TIPS
Golden Delicious apples produce a particularly fine and green juice. Out of season, any other sort can be used. Instead of wheatgrass, leafy vegetables such as young leaf spinach, beetroot leaves or baby leaf salad can also be used. It is important that they are of a good quality and are fresh.

Dried Fruit Salad

An oriental surprise

Preparation time
15 minutes + soaking
time overnight

Serves 4

200 g/1¼ cup mixed
dried fruit (dates, figs,
apricots, raisins, plums)
30 g/3 tbsp peeled
almonds
30 g/3 tbsp pine nuts
3 tbsp raw cane sugar
1 dash orange blossom
water
2 sprigs of mint

Cut the dried fruit into 1-cm/⅜-inch pieces and leave covered with water to soak overnight.

The next day, drain the soaked dried fruit. Put in a pan with the almonds, pine nuts, sugar and 250 ml/1 cup water. Bring to the boil and simmer on a low heat for a few minutes until the mixture has thickened.

Season the dried fruit salad with orange blossom water (do not use too much, as orange blossom water can quickly become the dominant flavour). Leave to cool gently.

Pluck the mint leaves. Arrange the dried fruit salad in small bowls or glasses and sprinkle with the mint leaves. The salad tastes good warm or cold.

TIP
This goes well with a refreshing lime and mint yoghurt. For this, mix and season soy yoghurt with a little lime juice and chopped mint.

Bircher muesli

The start of a great day!

Preparation time
30 minutes

Makes 1.3 kg/2 lb 14 oz,
serves 4

300 ml/1¼ cups vegan
whipping cream
150 ml/10 tbsp soy milk
150 ml/10 tbsp
unsweetened coconut
milk
2 tbsp raw cane sugar
Juice of 2 oranges,
freshly squeezed
150 g/5 oz mixed
wholemeal flakes
2 medium-sized apples
50 g/½ cup redcurrants
50 g/½ cup blueberries
150 g/1¼ cups
raspberries
100 g/1 cup blackberries
2 tbsp chia seeds

Put the whipping cream, soy milk, coconut milk, sugar, orange juice and mixed wholemeal flakes into a bowl, mix well and leave to infuse for 15 minutes.

In the meantime, wash the apples, remove the cores and grate. Carefully wash the berries, dry them, sort through and add to the wholemeal flakes mixture together with the grated apples. Mix well. Before serving, garnish with chia seeds.

TIPS
The muesli can also be prepared the evening before. Then, the following day, it may need to be thinned again with orange juice or soy milk. Depending on the season, other fruits can be used. In winter, a frozen berry mixture can be used and this can be added still frozen to the muesli; the muesli then has to be prepared the night before. Alternative sweeteners are maple syrup or agave syrup. Cinnamon, vanilla, dates or nuts can be added, if liked.

Fruit and Nut Bread

Perfect for a picnic

Preparation time
1 hour 30 minutes
(including baking time)

For 1 large loaf tin about
35 cm/14 inches in
length

150 g/1½ cups spelt flour
150 g/1½ cups buckwheat
or wholemeal flour
2 tbsp baking powder
100 ml/½ cup agave
syrup
400 ml/1½ cups rice milk
1 tsp ground cinnamon
1 pinch ground cloves
200 g/1¼ cups hazelnuts
150 g/1¼ cups walnuts
250 g/1¼ cups dried
apricots
200 g/1¼ cups dried
plums
250 g/1¼ cups dried figs
200 g/1¼ cups raisins
Vegetable margarine and
flour for the tin

Preheat the oven to 160°C/320°F. Grease the loaf tin with vegetable margarine and dust with flour.

Mix the two types of flour with the baking powder in a bowl. Add the agave syrup, rice milk, ground cinnamon and cloves and mix with the electric hand whisk into a smooth dough.

Cut the nuts up roughly. Cut the dried fruit into 1-cm/⅜-inch pieces. Add both to the dough and mix in.

Fill the greased loaf tin with the dough. Bake on the lowest level in the preheated oven for about 1 hour, covering with tin foil at the end if needed.

TIPS
The fruit and nut bread can be kept in the fridge, wrapped in cling film, for a long time. It can also be frozen. Oat, spelt or almond milk can be used as an alternative to the rice milk.

Papaya Lassi

The sister of the mango lassi

Preparation time
15 minutes

Makes 2 glasses of 250
ml/1 cup

1 very ripe papaya
Juice of 1 lime
200 g/¾ cup natural soy
yoghurt
100 ml/7 tbsp soy milk
1 pinch ground
cardamom
½ tsp garam masala

Peel the papaya, cut in half and remove the core. Roughly dice the fruit flesh and purée in a tall container with the hand blender. Season the papaya purée with the lime juice.

Mix the soy yoghurt, soy milk and cardamom in a bowl until smooth.

Add a third of the papaya purée to each of two glasses and fill up with the yoghurt drink. Dust with garam masala and serve.

TIP
If you would like it to be even fruitier, sweeten the papaya purée with 1 tbsp agave syrup. Instead of the papaya, the lassi can also be prepared with other fruits such as mango or raspberries. Then sprinkle with wheatgerm or chia seeds.

Matcha Iced Tea

An energy boost and a pick-me-up, good for concentration

Preparation time
40 minutes (including cooling time)

Makes about 1 litre/4¼ cups, serves 4

5 g/1 tbsp matcha tea powder
50 ml/4 tbsp elderflower syrup
30 ml/2 tbsp rose syrup
1½ tbsp freshly squeezed lime juice

Bring 1 litre/4¼ cups water to the boil and put in a bowl. Wait for a few minutes, then add the matcha tea powder, taking care that the water is no more than 80°C/175°F. Mix well with a whisk and allow to cool.

After cooling, add the remaining ingredients, mix well and pour into a carafe. Allow to cool completely in the fridge.

Before use, shake the matcha tea well, as the powder will sink to the bottom. The finished tea can be kept in the fridge for 2-3 days.

TIPS
The amount of matcha tea can be varied depending on how intense and herby you would like the taste to be. Matcha can be bought in any good tea shop. It is a high-value, ground Japanese green tea which is rich in amino acids and antioxidants and contains a lot of caffeine. Rose syrup is available online.

Rhubarb, Apple and Vanilla Juice

A declaration of love to spring

Preparation time
30 minutes + cooling time

Makes about 1 litre/4¼ cups, enough for 4 portions

2 stalks of rhubarb
2 pinches ground vanilla
2-3 tbsp raw cane sugar
2 apples (e.g. Gala)
2 tbsp elderflower syrup

Wash the rhubarb, remove the threads and cut into small pieces. Put into a small pan together with the vanilla, sugar and 300 ml/1¼ cups water and bring to the boil. Then cook for 4-6 minutes on a low heat until soft, stirring occasionally, and put in a food processor while still warm.

Wash the apples, cut into quarters, remove the core and add the apple quarters to the rhubarb, together with the elderflower syrup and 300 ml/1¼ cups water. Mix on the highest setting for 3 minutes. Pour into a carafe and allow to cool. Mix well again before serving.

TIP
If you have a juicer, the apples can be juiced and the water can be left out. The water is only needed so that the juice does not become too thick. If liked, season with lemon juice. If you prefer something a little sweeter, then increase the amount of elderflower syrup. The juice can be kept covered in the fridge for 2 days.

Vanilla Pancakes

The finishing touch to any weekend brunch

Preparation time
20 minutes

Serves 4

150 g/1¼ cups spelt flour
100 g/1 cup white flour
1 heaped tsp baking
powder
2 pinches salt
2 tbsp neutral-flavoured
vegetable oil
4 tbsp raw cane sugar
2 pinches ground vanilla
5-8 tbsp neutral-
flavoured vegetable oil
for frying

Add all the ingredients – except for the oil for frying – to a bowl together with 300 ml/1¼ cups water and mix with the hand blender until it forms an even batter. Leave the batter to rise for 10 minutes.

Lightly coat a non-stick pan with oil. Make pancakes from the batter and fry these on a medium heat on both sides until golden brown. Serve warm.

TIP
Add 100-150 g/½-¾ cup blueberries, forest fruits or finely chopped strawberries to the batter after mixing, if liked. The pancakes are also good when eaten cold.

Rooibos Cappuccino

We think it's even better than a regular cappuccino

Preparation time
10 minutes

Serves 4

12 g/2½ tbsp rooibos tea
200 ml/¾ cup almond
milk
1 pinch cocoa powder
1 pinch ground
cinnamon

Pour the rooibos tea into a tea infuser with 250 ml/1 cup hot water and leave to diffuse for at least 3-5 minutes. This makes the tea concentrate for 4 portions.

Beat 50 ml/3½ tbsp of almond milk per portion in the milk frother until frothy.

Remove the tea infuser and pour 50 ml/3½ tbsp of tea concentrate per potion into a coffee mug or tea cup. Carefully fold in the foamed milk and sprinkle with a little chocolate and cinnamon powder. Sweeten to taste.

TIP
The concentrated rooibos tea can also be made in large quantities and left in a bottle somewhere cool. The tea concentrate can be kept in the fridge for 5 days.

tibits

Hiltl

BASIC RECIPES

Practical kitchen elements: a helping hand for everyday vegan dishes

Every kitchen needs its little helpers, for example, to bind sauces, to stop cream from curdling or to thicken soups. Many of the popular, conventional products are made with animal substances, which is why the conversion to purely plant-based aids is essential here.

One of the best plant-based **gelling agents** is **agar agar,** which is made from red algae and firmly and reliably binds any dish when it is cooked with the other ingredients for at least three minutes. Agar agar is therefore suitable for a variety of preparations such as flans, puddings, terrines or cake glaze. As the products available can have considerably different gelling properties, it is important to follow the instructions carefully and weigh out the agar agar exactly. As a rule, substitute 10 grams/⅓ oz of pure agar agar for 12 sheets of gelatine.

Any uncertainties you may have using these gelling agents will vanish with frequent use – for example, irritation over the slight smell of the sea. This disappears after cooking. Also, the fact that the effect of the gel only manifests during cooling leaves many to doubt their success until the very last moment.

Alternatives to agar agar are **guar** or **locust bean gum**, with which sauces, soups, tart fillings or ice cream can be thickened easily. Also, the Asian binding agent kudzu, which is produced from the root of a climbing plant, is an effective alternative. While guar and locust bean gum only need to be stirred with a liquid and then they swell up of their own accord, the clumpy kudzu powder must be broken up before use and dissolved completely in water. The mixture is then stirred into the respective dish once it has been taken off the heat.

For light binding, nuts processed into pastes are also suitable, for example, the well-known sesame paste **tahini**, unsweetened **almond butter** or **cashew butter**. These can simply be stirred into soups, sauces, dressings and smoothies, and will then change their consistency and add a slightly nutty taste. Those who would like a stronger taste should try the **paste** from **poppy seeds, tiger nuts, pumpkin seeds** or **black sesame seeds.** When buying them, take care that the pastes are unsweetened and pure – in the supermarket in particular there are many sweetened and processed versions which we do not recommend.

Raw cane sugar, sugar beets and sugar cane also have a use in vegan cooking. As well as this, there is, however, a large range of delicious products which are worth trying: sweets which are made from fruits, such as thickened pear juice, date syrup or sugar beet syrup, birch sugar or stevia leaves. These can be used to prepare splendid dishes such as muesli, cakes, baked goods or fruit salads. Agave, maple or palm syrup can be used to sweeten tea, and are also good for pancakes, waffles or cocktails.

Spätzle

A much-loved German classic

Preparation time
30 minutes

Makes 1 kg spätzle,
enough for 4 portions

For the dough
250 g/1½ cups spätzle
flour (Spätzlemehl) or
durum wheat semolina
300 g/3 cups white flour
150 ml/10 tbsp rice milk
1 heaped tbsp salt
1 pinch ground nutmeg
1 pinch ground turmeric

Also
5 tbsp olive oil
Salt, ground pepper

Add the ingredients for the dough to a bowl along with 300 ml/1¼ cups water and mix well with your hands until a thick dough is formed. Leave the mixture to stand for about 5 minutes.

Push the mixture through a colander slowly into boiling, salted water. As soon as the spätzle float to the surface, lift them out and submerge in cold water. Allow to drain well and put to one side.

Just before serving, fry the spätzle in the oil until golden brown and season with salt and pepper.

TIPS
Depending on the type of flour and the moisture in the air, you may need more or less water. The mixture can also be scraped from a board into boiling water. The spätzle can be prepared a day in advance. Important: then mix the finished spätzle with oil so that they don't stick together.

Mashed Potatoes

Simple and quick to prepare, whether for cottage pie or as an accompaniment to other dishes

Preparation time
30 minutes

1.2 kg/2.6 lbs floury
potatoes
1-2 tbsp salt
250 ml/1 cup soy milk
4 tbsp vegan double
cream
2 tbsp olive oil
20 g/¾ cup vegetable
margarine
Salt, ground nutmeg

Peel the potatoes and cut in half or into quarters depending on the size. Cook in plenty of salted water until soft. Drain and leave to drip dry. Put the potatoes through a passe-vite or mash with a masher.

Heat the soy milk, double cream and olive oil in a pan. Add the warm mixture slowly to the potatoes and fold in carefully. Depending on the type of potatoes, you will need more or less liquid before a fluffy consistency is achieved. Add the margarine and season with salt and nutmeg.

TIP
Leave the potatoes to dry on a baking tray in the oven at about 80°C/175°F for 5-10 minutes before puréeing.

Tomato Pesto

An all-rounder

Preparation time
10 minutes

Makes 500 g/1.1 lb

4 cloves of garlic
150 g/5 oz sundried
tomatoes, in oil
120 ml/½ cup extra
virgin olive oil
8 tbsp sunflower oil
140 g/½ cup tomato
purée/paste
½ tsp ground galangal

Peel the garlic. Drain the sundried tomatoes. Mix all of the ingredients into a fine purée with a food processor. Put the pesto into jars and store in the fridge.

Vegetable Stock

For the perfect seasoning

Preparation time
2 hours

Makes 3½ litres/15 cups

½ savoy cabbage
2 carrots
1 fennel bulb
2 onions, peel on
1 red bell pepper
1 small leek
2 tomatoes
2 tbsp olive oil
1 tbsp black pepper corns
1 tbsp each of fennel and
cumin seeds
2 bay leaves
4 sprigs parsley
1 sprig each of rosemary
and thyme
1 tbsp herb salt

Wash and prepare all of the vegetables and cut into large pieces. Heat the oil in a tall saucepan. Glaze the carrots, fennel, onions, pepper, leek and tomatoes in the hot oil until lightly browned. Stir occasionally.

Add the savoy cabbage and the seasoning and fry until they begin to release an aroma. Add the sprigs of herbs and douse with 4 litres (17 cups) water. Bring evenly to boil and leave to simmer for 1-1½ hours.

Season with herb salt. Pour the stock through a sieve, pour into boiled glass bottles, seal immediately and leave to mature. The stock can be kept in the fridge, firmly sealed, for at least 2 weeks.

TIPS
This stock can be used as a base for soups or sauces and to thin other dishes. Use onions with the peel on to produce a lovely brown colour. The seasoning and herbs can vary depending on what the stock will be used for and any can be added and changed.

Olive Ciabatta

Home-made always tastes best

Preparation time
2½ hours (including time
to rise and bake)

Makes 10-12 rolls or 1
loaf

42 g/½ cup fresh yeast (1
packet)
1 kg/2.2 lbs spelt flour
3 tbsp natural soy
yoghurt
200 ml/¾ cup olive oil
2½ tsp salt
300 g/1½ cup black
olives, pitted
1 bunch each of
rosemary and thyme
3 tbsp black sesame
seeds

Also
2 tbsp olive oil for
brushing
2 tbsp each of black
sesame seeds and coarse
salt for sprinkling

Dissolve the yeast in 600 ml/2½ cups lukewarm water and leave to stand for 10 minutes. Put the flour in a bowl and form a hollow in the middle. Add the dissolved yeast and the water, the soy yoghurt, olive oil and salt, carefully knead in and leave the dough to stand for another 10 minutes.

Chop the olives finely. Pluck the rosemary needles and the thyme leaves and chop both finely. Add the chopped herbs, the olives and the sesame seeds to the dough and knead everything well with your hands. Cover the dough with a cloth and leave to rise for 1 hour at room temperature until it has doubled in volume.

Knead the dough once more, separate into tennis ball-sized pieces and form these into ciabatta rolls, arrange on a baking tray lined with baking paper and leave to rise for another 30 minutes. Preheat the oven to 180°C/355°F.

Brush the rolls with olive oil and sprinkle with sesame seeds and coarse salt. Bake in the middle of the preheated oven for 20-30 minutes. The ciabatta rolls are done if they sound hollow when tapped on the bottom.

TIPS
The ciabatta rolls are suitable for freezing. When you're ready to use them, bake the rolls straight from the freezer in the centre of the oven at 180°C/355°F for about 20 minutes. To make the finished rolls crispy, place a bowl of water at the bottom of the oven. The ciabatta rolls can be varied in any way: chopped nuts, sundried tomatoes or fried onions and other Mediterranean herbs such as basil, marjoram and parsley can be used.

Tofu Marinade

Gives tofu a great kick

Preparation time
5 minutes

Makes 150 ml/10 tbsp

80 g/¼ cup ketchup
25 g/1½ tbsp Dijon
mustard
20 ml/4 tsp soy sauce
1 pinch chilli powder
½ tsp spicy madras curry
powder
2 tsp salt
10 g/2½ tsp raw cane
sugar

Stir all of the ingredients together thoroughly.

Brush the product to be marinated, for example tofu, seitan, tempeh or vegetable pieces, with the marinade and leave to marinate overnight in the fridge.

Vegan Mayonnaise

Lighter than the original

Serves 8

WITH ALMOND BUTTER

Preparation time
5 minutes

200 ml/¾ cup mild olive oil
50 g/¼ cup crushed ice
1 tbsp white balsamic vinegar
1 tsp vegan mustard
2 tbsp unsweetened almond butter
Salt, ground white pepper

Put all of the ingredients – excluding the salt and pepper – in a tall mixing bowl. Mix together with the electric whisk held without moving for 30 seconds. Then mix with the electric whisk moving back and forth. The mayonnaise will be ready after 1 minute. Season with salt and pepper.

TIPS
Because of its relatively high water content, this mayonnaise has fewer calories than conventional types. It should be prepared fresh as over time it will thicken due to the almond butter.

WITH SOY MILK

Preparation time
40 minutes

200 ml/¾ cup soy milk
1 tbsp lemon juice
½ tsp guar gum
100 ml/7 tbsp neutral-flavoured vegetable oil
Salt, ground white pepper

Put the soy milk in a tall mixing bowl and allow to reach room temperature. Then add the lemon juice and leave to stand for 10 minutes until the soy milk curdles.

Add the guar gum and mix through well with the electric whisk for 30 seconds. Pour in the oil in thin streams and mix until the mayonnaise is creamy. Season with salt and pepper.

TIP
The mayonnaise will stay fresh, sealed in a screw-top jar, in the fridge for at least 2 weeks.

Vegan Sponge Mixture

Ideal for tiramisu and other desserts

Preparation time
20 minutes (including baking time)

Makes 1 spring-form pan of 20-cm/8-inch in diameter

½ unwaxed lemon
60 g raw cane/5 tbsp caster/superfine sugar
75 g/½ cup white flour
6 g/1½ tsp baking powder
80 ml/⅓ cup sparkling mineral water
2 tbsp neutral-flavoured vegetable oil
Vegetable margarine and flour for the tin

Preheat the oven to 185°C/365°F. Grease and flour the cake tin.

Wash the lemon in hot water, dry and grate the zest. Put ½ tsp lemon zest, the sugar, flour and baking powder in a bowl and mix for a few minutes with an electric hand whisk. Then add the mineral water and the oil and stir for a few minutes.

Fill the greased tin with the sponge mix and bake in the middle of a preheated oven for about 10 minutes. Allow to cool for a few minutes, then remove from the spring-form pan and continue as per the recipe you are using.

TIP
The vegan sponge mixture is a suitable alternative for sponge fingers for a vegan tiramisu. Or break up into pieces instead of the vegan biscuits for the silken tofu with berries dessert (page 146).

Hiltl and tibits:
A PORTRAIT

A love story

Hiltl and tibits are two restaurant groups that are very different but also wonderfully similar. Hiltl, a family business with a record-breaking history as the first vegetarian restaurant in the world. Haus Hiltl in Zurich, which was founded in 1898 by Ambrosius Hiltl as a 'home for vegetarians and an abstinence café', has been transformed into a culinary hub of the city, with a cookery school (Hiltl Academy) and seven restaurants in greater Zurich, among two in outdoor swimming areas. All of these combine contemporary, meat-free enjoyment with a relaxed attitude towards life, not least since Rolf Hiltl took over the company as the fourth generation in charge and broke a few of the taboos from the company's history. Since 1993, wine and cocktails have been served in the former abstinence café; and at night the restaurant is transformed into a night club. The concept of vegetarianism that was seen a century ago has developed hugely, the focus now being on healthy, discerning and responsible enjoyment.

tibits, in contrast, is a relatively new creation of three brothers: Christian, Daniel and Reto Frei, together with Rolf Hiltl, who opened their first restaurant in the Seefeld area of Zurich in 2000. Rolf Hiltl helps out with his wealth of experience and owns half of the business. tibits quickly established itself among the countless Seefeld restaurants because its vegetarian range was fresh, imaginative and international; in addition, its chic and attractive interiors were recognized by guests as being stylish, modern and inviting.

The decision only to serve vegetarian food was not difficult for the Frei brothers. All three, brought up in St Gallen in the Rhine Valley, have been vegetarians since they were eight years old and they see this way of life as a gain, rather than a loss – a fundamental consensus which is becoming more and more the norm in an era when food awareness is changing radically. tibits feeds a huge number of people who have turned away from the consumption of meat for environmental and moral reasons.

'We stand for joie de vivre, freshness, lightness, wellbeing and good karma,' says Christian Frei, and it is clear from the success of tibits that he and his brothers have struck a chord. The concept proved to be so successful that there are now thirteen tibits restaurants, three in Zurich, two in Bern, Basel and London, and one in Lausanne, Lucerne, St. Gallen, Winterthur, and Darmstadt.

Hiltl and tibits do not only share passion and dedication. The two family businesses regularly exchange ideas about new products, dishes and recipes and process their everyday experiences

The two family businesses regularly exchange ideas about new products, dishes and recipes and they process their everyday experiences together.

together. Both companies attract highly food-conscious customers, paving the way for constant, critical feedback which, in turn, is reflected in their regular joint meetings.

It has become clear to both companies that more and more guests want to eat vegan. 'Mere vegetarianism,' says Reto Frei, 'has increasingly been perceived as inconsistent.' And it was during their discussions about interesting, substantial vegan dishes that the idea of a cookbook came to the fore. 'We have had requests for good, vegan recipes more and more often from our customers,' says Rolf Hiltl, 'so we said to ourselves: okay, we will write a book, and let's do it together.'

Hiltl and tibits bring a cornucopia of culinary experience to this book. Rolf Hiltl, for example, together with his chefs, has found countless ways to convert dishes that traditionally contain meat into vegetarian or vegan delights. His 'Zurich stew' is legendary, just like his 'Hiltl tartar'. Meanwhile, tibits has worked on 'veganizing' Bircher muesli, which surely would have led to a riot in a country shaped by the milk business if the final product had not been so convincing. In spring 2013, Hiltl also opened a shop with Switzerland's first 'vegetarian butcher' next to its restaurant and vegan ingredients from this cookbook can be bought in the Hiltl shop, located right on the corner of Haus Hiltl.

At the same time, the Frei brothers and Rolf Hiltl look back on experiences they've shared since opening in 2008 in London, one of the taste capitals of the world. They have noticed from their guests that vegan food is gaining momentum and increasingly being seen as part of a trendy lifestyle.

When new vegan recipes are created at tibits, they are drawn from a very well-stocked larder. 'Everything is already in the garden and in nature,' says Daniel Frei, who wants to avoid the idea of a vegan dish as a mere meat replacement. Rolf Hiltl's many years of experience have combined with the vegan philosophies of Hiltl and tibits to create an exemplary and wide-ranging collection of recipes.

INDEX
OF RECIPES

Index of recipes

Index of ingredients

Hiltl – healthy enjoyment since 1898

Haus Hiltl – flagship
Restaurant, buffet, takeaway,
bar and meeting rooms
Sihlstrasse 28
8001 Zurich

Hiltl Academy
Cooking classes and events
Sihlstrasse 24
8001 Zurich

Hiltl Shop and vegetarian butchery
St Annagasse 18
8001 Zurich

Hiltl Club
St Annagasse 16
8001 Zurich

Hiltl Dachterrasse
Bahnhofstrasse 88
8001 Zurich

Hiltl Pflanzbar
Talstrasse 62
8001 Zurich

Hiltl Sihlpost
Europaallee 1A
8004 Zurich

Hiltl Langstrasse
Langstrasse 84
8004 Zurich

Hiltl at the Beach
Strandbad Mythenquai
Mythenquai 95
8002 Zurich

Hiltl at the Lake
Seebad Kilchberg
Seestrasse 205
8802 Kilchberg

Founded in 1898, Hiltl is the oldest vegetarian restaurant in the world according to Guinness World Records.

Today, the Zurich-based company with around 300 employees from 70 nations is managed by the Hiltl family's fourth generation: with healthy indulgence, gastronomic passion and responsibility towards the diverse creation of mankind, animals and nature.

At the headquarters on Sihlstrasse in the served à la carte restaurant with a buffet, bistro, take-away, seminar rooms, the Vegimetzg with the first vegetarian butchery in Switzerland and the Hiltl Academy, the competence centre for vegetarian and vegan indulgence, as well as outside the Hiltl flagship: in the Pflanzbar at Blumen Krämer near Paradeplatz, the roof terrace at the PKZ Women clothing store on Bahnhofstrasse, in the Sihlpost on Europaplatz near Zurich Main Station, on Langstrasse and during summer in two summer restaurants by Lake Zurich. On weekends you can dance through the night at the Hiltl Club.

The vegetarian and vegan delicacies, which are freshly prepared in the restaurant's own kitchen, can also be enjoyed at caterings and various events. Since 2009 Hiltl and SWISS have a tasty cooperation and passengers can enjoy our vegetarian delights as well as Hiltl «Special Meals» high above the clouds.

www.hiltl.ch

Previously published cookbooks:
Meat the Green (German, English, French)
Hiltl Virtuoso Vegetarian (German, English, French)
Hiltl Veggie International. A World of Difference (German, English)
Globi kocht vegi (German)
Greentopf (German)

tibits – fresh, enjoyable, uncomplicated

London
12–14 Heddon Street, off Regent Street
124 Southwark Street, near to Tate Modern

Basel
Meret-Oppenheim-Platz 1, next to the station
Stänzlergasse 4, adjacent to the Steinen

Lausanne
Place de la Gare 11, in the station

St. Gallen
Bahnhofplatz 1a, next to the station

Darmstadt
Eschollbrücker Straße 65, on the Alnatura Campus

Bern
Bahnhofplatz 10, in the railway station
Gurtengasse 3, near the parliament building

Lucerne
Zentralstrasse 1, in the railway station, 1st floor

Winterthur
Oberer Graben 48, near the Obertor

Zurich
Seefeldstrasse 2, near the opera house
Falkenstrasse 12, tibits in the NZZ Bistro
Tramstrasse 2, near Sternen Oerlikon

All restaurants are open daily.

The name 'tibits' comes from the English term 'titbits', meaning 'bite-sized delicacies'. Our restaurants are all about fresh, healthy and enjoyable food and drink.

The extensive food boat is in a class of its own: from salads, soups and sandwiches to hot dishes and desserts, there is something for everyone. From breakfast through to after-work drinks and your evening meal, there are 40 titbits on offer every day.

Everything is freshly made, by hand, several times a day. Flavourful and energy-packed dishes and colourful, nutritional, healthy, balanced meals. Guests create their own plate and then pay by weight, so they can take as much or as little as they want.

At tibits we value high-quality ingredients. Modified glutamates or genetically modified products do not enter our kitchen. In addition, nutritional information for each dish is clearly displayed so that our guests can eat without worrying about their personal dietary requirements.

Today, tibits invites foodies to feast at its restaurants in the heart of London and all over Switzerland. We also provide outside catering.

More about us, as well as tasty news and delicious online recipes can be found on our website.

www.tibits.ch

Previously published cookbook:
tibits at home. Stylish vegetarian cuisine
With 50 recipes to try at home, AT Verlag, 7th edition

New Internationalist

New Internationalist is an award-winning, independent media co-operative. Our aim is to inform, inspire and empower people to build a fairer, more sustainable planet.

We publish a global justice magazine and a range of books, both distributed worldwide. We have a vibrant online presence and run ethical online shops for our customers and other organizations.

Previously published cookbooks:
The Global Bakery
The Adventurous Vegetarian
Global Vegetarian Kitchen
The Immigrant Cookbook

newint.org/books

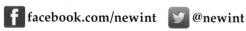 **facebook.com/newint** **@newint**